Theological & Grammatical Phrasebook of the Bible

Theological & Grammatical Phrasebook of the Bible

by

William White, Jr.

MOODY PRESS
CHICAGO

Library of Congress Cataloging in Publication Data
White, William, 1934-
    Theological & grammatical phrasebook of the Bible.

    Includes bibliographical references and indexes.
    1. Hebrew language, Biblical—Terms and phrases.
2. Greek language, Biblical—Terms and phrases.
3. Bible—Theology. I. Title. II. Title: Theological
and grammatical phrasebook of the Bible.
BS525.W55 1984   220.4'4   83-25842
ISBN 8024-0218-6

1 2 3 4 5 6 7 Printing/BC/Year 89 88 87 86 85 84

Printed in the United States of America

Contents

Foreword

Quite aside from being the repository of divine revelation, the Hebrew and Greek Scriptures are wonderfully artistic compositions in their own right. Two-thirds of the Old Testament, for example, is written in poetic form; the books of Job and Daniel follow an ancient Babylonian literary pattern, and the form of the gospel of John is based on that employed in the writing of countless tablets from Mesopotamia. Most translations into English, and especially the towering King James Version, have endeavored to reflect the literary artistry of the originals in the best possible ways. In the process they have preserved words and phrases that, although perhaps Semitic or Greek in origin, have long been adopted in their English form as a treasured and indeed normal part of our linguistic expression.

Certain of those terms, however, still need some explanation. How often have readers puzzled over expressions such as "for three transgressions and for four," "the seven stars and Orion," "maranatha," and "draw a bow at a venture"? In this book, those and many other expressions are explained in simple, uncomplicated language. Their origins are frequently traced to long-dead cultures, and the way that they have been understood through the centuries is described carefully.

The discussion of such theological terms as "kingdom of heaven," "Lord of hosts," and "only begotten Son" is marked by a high degree of scholarly objectivity. Attention is paid to the way in which the phrases are rendered by different English versions, and some of the entries have their own short bibliography that students can consult with profit.

This phrasebook is the product of careful scholarship and will undoubtedly prove to be a valuable reference work for all students of the Scriptures. It will do much to correct long-standing misinterpretations of the Hebrew and Greek texts, and will point the reader to the kind of understanding of the inspired Word that the original recipients possessed.

Wycliffe College, R. K. HARRISON
University of Toronto

Preface

The publisher and author would like to thank the following persons for their help in producing this book: Sara Jane White for hours of indexing and cross-referencing, Elizabeth Jane White for preparing the manuscript, Robert T. Tuten and Leonard J. Coppes for preliminary notes and suggestions on many of the words and phrases, and the staff of the Westminster Theological Seminary Library for highly professional help and the use of the collection of rare early Bibles and texts.

Introduction

All cultures both ancient and modern have a set of ideas about the cosmos, its origin, and man's place in it. Those ideas can be thought of as the culture's world view. That world view also includes priorities—what is most important and least important in that culture. The one human activity that most clearly communicates that world view is language. The words and phrases that the people of a culture use to express themselves are not only specific to their thoughts and emotions but, over time, come to define them. What is most important to a social group will be most important and most frequent in its language.

The various peoples of the Middle East are a clear example of this phenomenon. The Babylonian language as it has come down to us has innumerable words to describe omens, astrological signs, and soothsaying practices. Classical Arabic has well over one hundred words to describe the conditions and ages of camels, while classical Greek produced an extensive vocabulary of political, social, and philosophical terms. The revelation of God in the Scripture was given in specific terms that had specific cultural associations and linguistic forms. Although there has been a good deal of interest in word studies over the past fifty years, culminating in multivolume sets of books on Old Testament and New Testament word studies, there has been considerable less attention paid to the phrase formations of the Bible. The phrase is the next level of meaning and complexity for the Bible student.

The *Theological and Grammatical Phrasebook of the Bible* is a new kind of reference work. It seeks to go beyond the available lexicons and word studies and deal with the more extended associations of words that we call phrases. Basically, a phrase is a group of two or more words bearing certain grammatical associations that influence their usage or meaning. As the student compares phrase with phrase, patterns of usage and meaning structures will begin to become evident. However, this is something of a first pioneering effort. It will undoubtedly have imperfections in understanding and flaws in explanation, but the author's hope is that it will introduce both student and teacher to a new way of approaching the study of the English Bible, helping them gain insight into the original text and the processes of historical translation.

This is not an exhaustive volume, nor is it meant to be. It is a guide to understanding how biblical phrases are put together and used to convey meaning in the text, and it teaches by examples. The phrases discussed are chosen from three categories:

1. Phrases of great importance to biblical theology. These are statements that are the sum and substance of the Christian life and teaching and that guide the believer. Phrases such as "Ye must be born again" and "only begotten Son" are phrases through which the heart of the gospel is conveyed.

2. Phrases that illustrate important aspects of biblical semantics or meaning and the thought patterns that lie behind Hebrew and Greek speech. Among such phrases are "King of kings and Lord of lords" and "for three . . . and for four."

3. Phrases used only once in Scripture that are difficult to understand and enlightened only by more recent Semitic and Hellenistic studies and the discoveries of archaeology. This category includes such examples as "dove's dung" and "seven stars and Orion."

Certain editorial decisions were made in presenting the material that require explanation. The first concerns the author's viewpoint of the inspiration and inerrancy of Scripture, a basic consideration when anyone writes about the Bible. Without any qualification whatsoever the author adheres to the verbal inspiration of the Old and New Testaments as the complete Word of God.

The second decision was to use the King James Version (KJV) as the base text. The fact is that the overwhelming majority of English Bible students have first read and memorized the texts from the venerable KJV. Once learned as a child or as a convert to Jesus Christ, the words of Scripture are for most people the words of the KJV. They are part of the individual's vocabulary and piety, so that no matter how many other versions the student may subsequently read or memorize, the one programmed into his mind is usually the KJV; it becomes a permanent portion of the memory.

So the KJV, replete with its great majesty of language and mistakes in translation, and pouring out its torrent of obsolete words and constructions, is still the easiest for the English-speaking layman to recall. For that reason the KJV is the base text used in this study. However, a number of contemporary versions are quoted with each phrase. No qualitative judgments are made on any version, but it will become clear to the reader which of them present the most incisive readings of the original Hebrew and Greek and which prefer to paraphrase in an attempt for a more modern form.

The third choice was in regard to the transliteration of Hebrew and Greek characters. Although the equivalence of Greek characters in English is well established and not complicated, the indication of the sounds of Hebrew is never easy in English script because of an underlying problem. The Hebrew writing system is not an alphabet but a syllabary, which means that each sign represents not just a vowel or a consonant but a vowel plus a consonant or a consonant plus a vowel, even if one of the two is silent or barely audible. For that reason only approximations of the sounds of Hebrew can be given. Though the system used in this book will not satisfy the needs or standards of all scholars, Hebrew transliteration is based on that used in *Theological Wordbook of the Old Testament* (Moody Press, 1980), 2 volumes.

Transliteration of the tetragrammaton (YHWH), representing the Hebrew covenant name for God (Yahweh, or Jehovah), and usually rendered "LORD," is always shown in the articles without vowels—as *YHWH* or *yhwh*.

The last decision was that lower critical problems would be largely omitted; that is, they are not discussed and the text accepted is not defended. This book is not the forum for that type of argument. An arbitrary choice was made to use the standard edition of the Hebrew text, R. Kittel, ed., *Biblia Hebraica* (Stuttgart, 1954), and one of the most widely used editions of the New Testament text, E. Nestle, ed., *Novum Testamentum Graece et Latine* (Stuttgart, 1963).

Entries are listed alphabetically by the words printed in bold type—which in a few instances are preceded by words in light type in order to give the full phrase. Scripture references after the English entry indicate a major (and sometimes the only) location of the phrase. References in brackets (e.g., [H v. 7]) indicate location in the Hebrew Scriptures when it differs from the English.

THE BASIC STRUCTURE OF BIBLICAL LANGUAGE

1. *The text.* The Old Testament was written from about 1500 to 400 B.C., in the Hebrew language, and on scrolls made from animal skins. Hebrew is a round syllabic script derived by western Semites from the Middle Egyptian hieroglyphs. In addition, Daniel 2:4b-7:28, Ezra 4:8-6:18; 7:12-26, and Jeremiah 10:11 have survived in the Aramaic language, an eastern Semitic dialect that was a common trade language of the Persian period. Both Hebrew and Aramaic are Semitic languages and so are very different in structure and vocabulary from the Indo-European languages such as Greek, Latin, French, German, and English. It is often a trying and difficult task to carry over the thought forms and levels of meaning in Hebrew or Aramaic—developed as they were in an agricultural, paternalistic, and theocratic society—into the speech of modern urban man.

Though Greek appears to be simpler than Hebrew, it is even more exacting to translate its multiplicity of moods, tenses, and particles into coherent and accurate English. No matter how many ancient documents are consulted or how many parallel usages sought out, sooner or later the student is faced with what Nigel Turner has labeled "Christian words." These are Greek words that are totally dependent for their meaning in the New Testament on contexts in the Old Testament. Though they are Greek in form and function, they are given new and fuller meanings in the setting forth of the gospel of salvation in the atonement of Jesus Christ for sin. For that reason it is not enough simply to collect and catalog all of the occurrences and meanings of a Greek word in the classical and nonliterary papyri. It is of central importance to examine the term in its grammatical context both in the Scriptures and in its secular occurrences. The inflected forms of a word—that is, the range of endings the word carries— its syntax or functional relationship to the other words it is used with, and its specific addition or subtraction of emphasis in the context are the considerations explored in this work. These features are also compared to the parallel constructions and translations of other major versions—ancient, medieval, and modern.

2. *The transmission of the text.* The transmission of the text of the Bible has been from one language, culture, and age to another. Since that process is obviously linguistic, it is necessary to examine major translations, the languages and cultures they represent, and their impact on subsequent translations.

The Hebrew Bible in its three great divisions (the law, the prophets, and the writings) is by no means a homogeneous and uniform product. It was written over a period of probably more than one thousand years and contains poems, episodes, literary asides, and allusions that may be two thousand years older than their written forms. Vocabulary, forms, and even syntax vary to some degree from book to book and from one period of the language to another. The Hebrew of 2 Chronicles, for example, is not the Hebrew of Job. When the rich panoply of themes and styles was translated, the differences were abraded toward homogeneity by the very process and requirements of translation. Often a new effort at sublimity introduced some incomprehensibility, the best example being The Song of Songs (Song of Solomon) in most translations. The treatment received by that inspired poem of love bounded by God's law illustrates the Napoleonic dictum "From the sublime to the ridiculous is but a step."

The evidence is rather clear that the Hebrew Bible possibly was edited at several points in antiquity in order to make certain obscure words and forms more meaningful. It is also evident that many of the ancient literary allusions of the Hebrew text were lost on the generations of Jews who returned to Palestine after the captivity. However, with the recovery and decipherment of cuneiform tablets in Sumerian, Akkadian, Elamite, Ugaritic, and now Eblaite, some words and phrases veiled for centuries are taking on life and meaning that had been lost for over three thousand five hundred years.

As the people of Israel moved through history from their tight-knit rural villages into the cosmopolitan world of the Greeks, they lost contact with the oral, and later the aural, traditions of the Hebrew language. Jews living in the Diaspora (or Dispersion) in places such as Babylon and Egyptian Elephantine used Aramaic exclusively in their daily lives and synagogue services. Though Aramaic was very much a Semitic language, Greek certainly was not. And Greek literature had a tradition as old and varied as that of Hebrew (King David the psalmist and Homer the poet were near contemporaries). The cultural struggle that developed between the old, Semitic East and the new, Greek

West lasted for three-and-a-half centuries, from Alexander's conquests of 330 B.C. until the fall of Jerusalem to Titus in A.D. 70.

One positive outcome of this struggle was the production of the Septuagint, a Greek translation of the Old Testament. This version has come down to us as the result of a crazy-quilt of many attempts to translate the Hebrew Bible into Greek. But the Judaism reflected in the Greek Old Testament was not that reflected in the Hebrew Old Testament. The Jews of the Hebrew Bible lived in a compacted village society, which was patriarchal and monolithic, and their religion and language reflected those facts. But the Jews of the Greek Bible lived in an open and troubled society, one in which science was being born and over which the Hellenistic goddess Tyche, "Lady Luck," held sway. But the Septuagint, of limited but nonetheless important value for the study of the Hebrew text, served as a bridge between the Old and New Testaments. The words and phrases of the Septuagint appear in a continuous stream from Matthew to Revelation. In fact, no reference Bible ever published has isolated them all. To a large degree the New Testament verbalization of the Old Testament text is that of the Greek version. That is not to imply that the New Testament writers were ignorant either of the Hebrew Bible or the Aramaic Targums or translations. It simply means that the Greek version (Septuagint) was their primary Old Testament text. For example, the New Testament makes no attempt to carry across the many marvelous titles and names of God so common in the Hebrew Bible, except for a few distinct usages. For the most part, it simply uses the common Hellenistic Greek title *kurios* ("Lord"). Whether this indicates more emphasis on God's immanence and less on His transcendence must be left for the theologians to decide, but there is no doubt that it is a significant and indeed profound change—and only one of many.

The next fundamental change in the biblical text came with the appearance of the Latin Vulgate and the subsequent rise of Western Christianity. In a situation similar to the rise of the Septuagint, a host of attempts were made within the first two centuries of the church to produce Latin versions, some from Hebrew and others from Greek. The tradition of those translations, whether partial or complete, is termed the "Old Latin Version." Finally, in the fourth century A.D. Pope Damasus I commissioned Jerome to produce a standardized text of the Latin Bible. About A.D. 400 the Vulgate or "Common" version was produced and soon became both the dominant text in Western Christendom and the premier literary work of the entire medieval period. Its importance to later translations lies in its being the subliminal, memorized text of the early translators of the various versions in the European languages, and of the sixteenth-century Reformers. Over the centuries it excluded all other versions in the West, and most of the population of Europe never knew there had ever been a Hebrew or Greek original until the beginning of the Renaissance.

Like all of the vestiges of the Roman Republic and Empire, the Latin Vulgate had a profound impact on later generations. Even in the most modern and contemporary versions many of the basic terms or equivalents of the Vulgate still appear. Terms such as *justification, sanctification, propitiation, glorification, dedica-*

tion, and many others passed into the everyday vocabulary of the Christian church through the Vulgate—so much so that the New Testament of the King James Version is probably more Roman than Greek! Since the appearance of the KJV, the Protestant churches have lost the historical connection with the Vulgate tradition, and its impact on the Reformation era is largely overlooked. But when a close study is made to determine why English versions from Wycliffe in 1340 to the KJV in 1611 have certain ways of expressing the Greek original, the conclusion is that the translation was often made out of deference to the Vulgate. Explaining the phrases of the King James Version, *Living Bible, New International Version, New American Standard Bible, New King James Version,* or any other English version requires two things. First we must elucidate the meaning of the original text in the context of its time and place. Second, we must seek to explain by what chain of logic or happenstance the English phrase came to be as we read it. Amazingly enough, that second exercise (not often taught in classrooms) will usually illumine the first. Some versions, not often quoted, but of importance in the transmission of the text from one language to another, are mentioned in this book. Citations to them are given in the bibliography.

3. *The task of exegesis.* This is not a commentary or a work of exegesis but a book of explanation. It is designed to take up the study of Scripture where the lexicons, dictionaries, and wordbooks leave off. But to use it properly and to learn its lessons and go beyond them, several of the elements discussed in the body of the work should be understood. Three of those will occur repeatedly: the construct-chain of Hebrew nouns and adjectives, the stem structure of the Hebrew verbal system, and the tense and mood system of the Greek verb. Several other less complex features of the two languages are also included. For greater ease of comprehension, a brief synopsis follows. These paragraphs will be referred to frequently in the discussion of individual phrases.

One feature of Hebrew grammar frequently mentioned in this book is the genitive, called the construct chain. The words associated in this construction are said to be in the construct state. In most of the languages with which we are familiar, the genitival relationship is usually expressed by means of a preposition: "word *of* Moses," "parola *di* Moise" (Italian), or "woord *van* Mozes" (Dutch). It may also be expressed by changing the last letter or part of the second of the two words so that what was the object of the preposition *of* in English, *di* in Italian, or *van* in Dutch is put into a special case called the *genitive.* For example, "word of Moses" becomes *verbum Mosi* in Latin and *rhēma Mōuse-ōs* in Greek. But in Hebrew the *first* word is altered. In many cases, that alteration is shown only by a shift of the accent, which is seen in the intensity of the vowel or stress on the vowel. Thus "word of Moses," made up of "word" (Hebrew *dabar*) and "Moses" (Hebrew *Mōsheh*) when combined in the construct becomes "word-of-Moses" (Hebrew *dᵉbar Mōsheh*) or, more exactly, "word-of Moses." Many familiar phrases in English Bibles represent this construction in the Hebrew.

Hebrew verbs also do not follow the familiar patterns of Indo-European verbs. Hebrew verbs have no clear tense forms indicating past, present, or future. Instead, they have a series of "stems," each with a different emphasis. When Medieval Hebrew grammarians began to examine and describe the structure of Hebrew, the only other Semitic language that had already developed a literature of self-examination was Arabic. Because the Arabs had followed the custom of the ancient Greeks and had written about their language and its features, the terms that came to be used to describe Hebrew were Arabic, and later Latin.

For our purposes it is best to say that the Hebrew verb has no tenses but two *aspects,* past and nonpast. Depending on the context, the past form can mean both past and under certain circumstances even future, while the nonpast is a present and imperfect. Though the aspects are only two in number, they can be combined and alternated to produce a wide variety of meanings.

But there are a number of verb stems. The basic, or ground, stem can be altered into a series of derived stems, whose major forms and meanings are shown in the following table. The classic Hebrew illustrative or paradigm verb is *qāṭal,* "to kill."

Name of Stem	Form	Meaning
Qal (ground stem)	qatal	to kill
Nif-'al (ordinary passive)	niqtal	to kill oneself
Pi-'el (active intensive)	qittel	to kill many, to massacre
Pu-'al (passive intensive)	quttal	to be massacred
Hif-'il (active causative)	hiqtiyl	to cause to kill
Hof-'al (passive causative)	hoqtal	to cause to be killed
Hithpa-'el (reflexive intensive)	hithqattel	to kill oneself

Note that the three basic consonants (*q, ṭ,* and *l*) are separated by vowels and are sometimes doubled in the different alignments. But they never change their order, which is always *q + ṭ + l*. There are a few other stems but they occur rarely.

Generally, Greek tenses are not strictly the same as those in English, in that they refer to the specific point of an action in relation to what came before or is about to come after. The aorist, for example, only describes a single action in time, the action of a single moment. Therefore an aorist command or prayer (and most prayers in the New Testament are in the aorist) usually states no general and everlasting principle, but only *the state of the action at that time.*

Thus grammarians call the aorist *punctiliar* (or "single pointed") rather than *durative* ("lasting") or *iterative* ("repeated"). Nigel Turner expresses the situation well in discussing Jesus' illustration from the lilies: "Indeed, it often involves the initiation of action that has not yet begun, as when Jesus enjoined his disciples to 'consider the lilies of this field.' They were walking in the countryside but had not observed the tiny flowers until he drew their attention to them.

His exclamation on this particular occasion was meant for that occasion only. 'Look! You have not yet noticed the lilies in this field! Consider them now!'" (*Grammatical Insights into the New Testament* [Edinburgh: T & T Clark, 1965], 30.)

The Greek verb has more forms and is more precise in the use of them than English or even German. A brief table will explain:

Greek Tenses

Name	Description	Example
Present	action proceeding in present	*graphō* "I am writing"
Imperfect	action proceeding in past	*egraphon* "I was writing"
Perfect	action completed in present	*gegrapha* "I have written"
Pluperfect	action completed in past	*egegraphē* "I had written"
Aorist	action simply taking place in past	*egrapsa* "I wrote"
Future	action in the future	*grapsō* "I will write"
Future perfect	action to be completed in the future	*gegrapsetai* "It will have been written"

Perhaps a slight change of perspective will make the system clearer:

Action proceeding:	Imperfect	Present	Future
Action simply taking place:	Aorist	——	Future
Action completed:	Pluperfect	Perfect	Future perfect

The most interesting of the tenses is the aorist, which has no direct equivalent in English and which has very precise application in many New Testament passages.

Greek not only has an active and passive voice like English, but also a middle voice, which generally expresses the idea that the subject performs an action upon himself or for his own benefit. There is also a fully developed system of modes, or moods, that show the degree of certainty of an action, or the relation of one set of certainties to another. The moods include the indicative, subjunctive, optative, imperative, infinitive, and participial.

Meanings of moods have to be defined to a large extent by context, but certain forms lost their sharp distinctions over the centuries. The most important Greek moods in the New Testament are the indicative, subjunctive, infinitive, and participial, although both the optative and imperative are also used.

One other important grammatical feature is the Greek genitive. It is an inflected case—that is, it is indicated by a change of the ending on a noun, pronoun, or adjective. The genitive construction is the primary way to show possession, and it specifically limits the use of the noun in a phrase. A typical genitive construction is behind "the Son of man" (Matt. 16:27). The Greek is *ho huios tou anthrōpou*, the literal meaning of which is "the-son-the(of)-man(of)."

The second article and the second noun both have the *ou* ending that marks the genitive.

Many points of Greek grammar bear on the proper interpretation of Greek phrases in the New Testament, and no doubt scholars differ on many of them. This book will point out some of the more important instances and how they affect the meaning of the text. Other writers may sincerely differ and with good evidence. But simply understanding the arguments involved should strengthen the reader's understanding of Scripture.

As explained above, the Septuagint (Greek) version of the Old Testament and the Latin Vulgate of the Old and New Testaments are the great historical intermediaries standing between the Hebrew and Greek originals and the English versions since Wycliffe's translation of 1340. But modern biblical scholarship has been bifurcated on very artificial lines. At the turn of the century Old Testament and New Testament studies, with the languages basic to both, were divided arbitrarily into separate departments and faculties. The practice began in Germany and after the First World War spread to the United States. When the two great evangelical scholars J. Gresham Machen and Oswald T. Allis went to Germany they studied under totally different faculties. But there is no reason why that false division should continue, and that is why this book discusses phrases in both testaments. The other way this book seeks to mend the rift is by considering constructs larger than single words. We must examine grammatical connections—phrases and even sentences—in order to rightly divide the Word of truth.

A

1
all the world should be taxed (Luke 2:1)
GREEK: *apographesthai pasan tēn oikoumenēn*

This familiar phrase appears in the narrative of the birth of Christ in Luke 2:1. It is a brief but eloquent summary of the edict of Caesar Augustus, the founder and first emperor of the Roman Empire. The verb *apographē* refers to a list or inventory of the names or families of persons and their relationships for purposes of taxation. The intent was definitely to take a census, but because that census was for tax purposes, the actual intent of the action, its ultimate goal, is properly represented by the KJV. The precise meaning of the words, however, is better translated by the more modern versions. The term *pasan* is the regular Greek adjective for "all" and refers to the entirety of the empire. The word *tēn* is the definite article and the noun *oikoumenēn* is the much-used term for world, specifically "the inhabited world," the world of human beings.

The enrollment or census of the empire mentioned in Luke 2:1 was initiated by Augustus's edict in about 7 B.C., but it was not actually carried out in Judea until some time after that. This is one reason so many scholars have set the birth of Jesus earlier than 4 B.C. (the date of the edict and the death of Herod in April of 4 B.C. set the parameters for the date of Jesus' birth). The fact that Mary and Joseph were required to travel to Bethlehem for the census may indicate that Joseph was at least prosperous enough—that is, had sufficient property—to be taxable under Roman law.

NASB: a census be taken
NIV, LB: a census should be taken
NKJV: all the world should be registered
RSV: all the world should be enrolled

Nigel Turner, *Christian Words* (Nashville: Nelson, 1981), pp. 501-2.

2
amen / verily (Num. 5:22; Matt. 5:18)
HEBREW: *'āmēn*
GREEK: *amēn*

A unique adverb that may have become over the centuries the best known Hebrew word in Scripture. Although it is a single word, its use developed into a virtual phrase of assent. It appears first in Num. 5:22, where it was required to be spoken twice by a woman accused of infidelity as she underwent trial by ordeal. In the Old Testament it was often used to signify agreement and obligation to the terms of a covenant—spoken as an affirmative response by both parties.

'Āmēn appears four times in the Psalms, at the end of each of the first four collections (41:13; 72:19; 89:52; and 106:48). In each case it is the congregational response of praise, and that usage became primary in the New Testament. It was first part of the service of the synagogue and later of the Christian church. Strange as it may seem, the Greek translation of the Old Testament, the Septuagint (LXX), actually shows several attempts to translate the Hebrew term *'āmēn*, but virtually every other version has retained the actual Hebrew and merely transliterated it. Jesus used the Greek form at the end of the Lord's Prayer, and it is found at the end of a number of the epistles. The word is used 101 times in the New Testament—50 times in John's gospel and 10 times in the Revelation. It may have been a unique feature of Jesus' speech. The major versions render the word (or phrase of which it is a part) in various ways, depending on the context.

NASB, RSV: Amen / truly
NIV: So be it / I tell you the truth
NKJV: Amen / assuredly
LB: Yes, let it be so / with all earnestness

3
angel of the Lord (Gen. 16:7; Matt. 1:20)
HEBREW: *mal'ak yhwh*
GREEK: *aggelos kuriou*

This phrase is used for the first time in Gen. 16:7, where the angel of the Lord appears to Hagar after she has fled from Sarai's harsh treatment. The phrase consists of two words: the common noun for "messenger," which appears some 213 times in the Old Testament, and the most sacred name of God among the Jews, Yahweh, often given in English versions as Jehovah. The "angel of the Lord" is always referred to in the masculine singular.

In many passages (Gen. 16:7; 22:11; Ex. 3:2; Judg. 6:11; 13:21; and others) the angel of the Lord is accorded such a transcendent position that he has the authority of God Himself. Thus many of these appearances are termed "theophanies," a Greek term meaning appearances or manifestations of the deity. Some theologians see the theophanies as appearances of the preincarnate Christ.

The phrase was taken directly over into Greek in the Septuagint, where the word for *messenger* was used to represent its Hebrew equivalent. However, a great and significant change was made with the sacred and unspeakable name of *Yahweh*. The Greek text translates it with the very common noun *kurious,* meaning "lord" or "master." That term was first used for the deity in oriental Greek and became commonplace in later centuries. From the Greek for "messenger" (*aggelos,* pronounced *ang-gelos*), the English word *angel* is derived through the Latin and appears in virtually all other languages. All modern versions read "angel of the Lord" in those passages.

The New Testament appearances of the phrase "angel of the Lord" are limited to three contexts:

1. The announcement of Jesus' birth (Matt. 1:20, 24; 2:13; Luke 1:11 (Gabriel, v. 19)
2. The resurrection (Matt. 28:2)
3. A number of episodes in Acts relating to the apostolic evangelization

All the versions cited read "angel of the Lord" in the New Testament passages, except the LB, which has only "angel."

4
ark of the covenant (Jer. 3:16)
  HEBREW: *'ārôn bᵉrît*

The Ark of the Covenant was the most sacred visual object in Old Testament worship. The command to construct it and the first mention of the Ark occur in Ex. 25:10. The phrase appears some 195 times in the Old Testament, mostly in the historical books and once in the prophets (Jer. 3:16). The word *'ārôn* specifically refers to a chest or box and is first used in Scripture for the sarcophagus of Joseph in the last part of Genesis: "And they embalmed him, and he was put in a coffin in Egypt" (50:26). The dimensions of the Ark of the Covenant are given in Ex. 25:10 as approximately four feet by two and one-half feet—a quite portable size.

The other term, *berît*, occurs some 280 times in the Old Testament and has several meanings, depending on the context. But the notion of covenant as the legal deposition made and presented by God for human redemption is prominent. The phrase suffers from some confusion because the same English word *ark* is used for the Hebrew term *tēbâ*, derived possibly from some other Semitic language and meaning "vessel" or "boat." It is used of both the ark of Noah in the Flood narrative of Genesis 6—8 and of the reed vessel in which the infant Moses was floated on the Nile (Ex. 2:3). It is unfortunate that the translators of the KJV saw fit to use the same English word for both the vessel of Noah and the sacred chest covered with gold that held the tablets of the Mosaic law, the showbread, and Aaron's rod that had budded.

The Ark of the Covenant is mentioned twice in the New Testament (Heb. 9:4; Rev. 11:19). In the book of Hebrews the Greek word *diathēkē* ("covenant") is the same one usually translated "testament"—as in the New Testament. That translation seems most appropriate, because the Ark of the Covenant was the most central and symbolic item of the Temple and of the whole Old Testament revelation of salvation. It is unfortunate that this very strong connection between the Old and New Covenants is obscured by so many of the modern translations, especially since the term *covenant* is so filled with meaning in biblical revelation.

NASB, NIV, NKJV, RSV: ark of the covenant
LB: Ark of God's covenant

B

Baal and Ashtaroth (Judg. 2:13)
HEBREW: *ba'al w^elā'ashtārôt*

This phrase (see Judg. 2:13; 10:6; 1 Sam. 7:4; 12:10) links the titles of male and female pagan deities widely worshiped by the Semites of the ancient Near East. The Eastern Semite form of the title *Ba'al,* which is *beli* ("lord"), has been found on tablets from Ebla dated to about 2,000 B.C. After the Exodus and the conquest of the land of Canaan, the Israelites came into direct conflict with the religion and culture of the pagan inhabitants. That cultural struggle was to continue almost to the end of the Old Testament era. The title *Astaroth* is more difficult to trace, as goddesses were always seen as the "lady" of a certain lord. Two attributes of the agriculture cults are present in the literature of virtually all ancient Near East societies: (1) the fertility of local men, animals, and crops was under the authority or ownership of the local *Ba'al* ("lord") and Ishtar/Astarte (his "lady"), and (2) the favor of those deities was obtained by rituals of sympathetic magic involving dances, inebriation, and various forms of sexual activity, including homosexuality. The rituals were assigned a greater efficacy depending on their grossness and depravity, the underlying idea being that no sacrifice was too great for the favor of the gods.

The ultimate act was the sacrifice of a family's firstborn child, as a number of ancient texts make clear. For example, a passage in the Babylonian religious poem "The Lament of the Righteous Sufferer" (*Ludlul Bel Nemeqi*) explains the pagan idea of the revulsion to human sensibilities of divine demands:

> I taught my countrymen to observe the god's rites,
> Instructed my people to value his name.
> As if a deity, I praised the king,
> Respect for the palace, the people I taught.
> Would that I knew that these were acceptable to my god,
> For what is right for oneself is a crime to a god,
> What one considers a disgrace, to a god is good.

Herodotus makes a similar observation about the sacred prostitution in the temple of Babylon:

A woman who has once taken her seat is not allowed to return home until one of the male visitors throws a silver coin into her lap, and takes her with him beyond the holy ground. When he throws the coin he says these words—"The goddess Mylitta prosper you." The silver coin may be of any size; it cannot be refused, for that is forbidden by the law, since once thrown it is sacred. The woman goes with the first man who throws her money, and rejects no one. When she has gone with him, and so satisfied the goddess, she returns home, and from that time forth no gift however great will prevail with her. (*The History,* #199)

So worship and participation in the Canaanite cult not only involved idolatry, the turning of one's back on the true God, but also debasing and disgusting rituals. Ashtaroth is a plural Canaanite form of Ishtar, the Babylonian fertility goddess. In some Babylonian literature the plural is used with the simple meaning of "goddess." For that reason the phrase may well be understood as "lord and ladies" or even "gods and goddesses."

NASB: Baal and the Ashtaroth
NIV, NKJV: Baal and the Ashtoreths
RSV: the Baals and the Astaroth
LB: Baal and the Ashtaroth idols

6

be born again (John 3:3)
GREEK: *gennēthēi anōthen*

In His discourse with Nicodemus (John 3:3-7), Jesus twice repeats the phrase "be born again." The notion of being "born of God" is repeated in 1 John, but nowhere else in the New Testament. The phrase consists of a complex verb form, the aorist subjunctive (which infers an action simply taking place in the past) in the passive voice of the common Greek verb "to be born," and an adverb of place.

The precise force of the second word in the phrase is interesting to examine. The adverb *anōthen* can mean "from above." That idea is foremost in John 19:11, where Jesus addresses Pontius Pilate and says, "You would have no authority over Me, unless it had been given you *from above*" (NASB, italics added). The double meaning "from above/again" is stressed in John 3. Unfortunately, that is extremely difficult to bring out in an English translation. Wycliffe's translation of 1380 reads "be born a newe," but Cranmer's translation of 1539 reads "be born from above." Modern versions have mostly followed the KJV, which followed Wycliffe.

NASB, NIV, NKJV: is (be) born again
RSV: is (be) born anew
LB: are born again

7
Beelzebub the prince of the devils (Matt. 12:24)
GREEK: *Beelzeboul archonti tōn daimoniōn*

This New Testament phrase (Matt. 12:24; Mark 3:22; Luke 11:15; the name itself appears alone in Matt. 10:25; 12:27; Luke 11:18-19) is based on Hebrew usage in the Old Testament. This pagan Canaanite god appeared in the cult of the Philistines at Ekron in the narrative of Ahaziah's accident and death (2 Kings 1:2-3, 6, 16). The name of the god is made up of two components—*ba'al* and *zebub*, or "lord of the flies." Both of the *b*'s in the word *zebub* are pronounced as a *v*, thus imitating in onomatopoetic form the buzzing of flies. Small golden cultic flies have been recovered from the excavations of Canaanite sites. In the traditions of the Jews the title Baalzebub became a name for Satan. However, as with many of the ancient pagan titles, the sound of the word was altered to an obscenity, so that Baalzebub became Baalzebul or Beelzebul ("lord of the dung"). The term is used by Jesus in Matt. 12:27 as it was applied to Him by the Jewish leaders.

Part of the confusion in spelling has come about because the Old Latin, Syriac, and Latin Vulgate versions disregarded the Greek, which clearly reads *Beelzebul*, and reverted back to the Old Testament Hebrew, which reads *Baalzebub*. The noun in apposition in the phrase is simply the general term *archōn* ("ruler"), as in the description of Nicodemus, who is said to be "a ruler (*archōn*) of the Jews" (John 3:1). The difficulty in properly understanding the play on words with the use of "lord of the dung" is reflected by the modern versions.

NASB: Beelzebul the ruler of the demons (note: "Beezebul"; "Beelzebub")
NIV: Beelzebub, the prince of demons (note: "Beezeboul" or "Beelzeboul")
NKJV: Beelzebub, the ruler of the demons
RSV: Beelzebul, the prince of demons
LB: Satan, king of devils (note: Lit., "Beelzebub")

8
Behold the Lamb of God (John 1:29)
GREEK: *ide ho amnos tou theou*

More than any other author of the New Testament, John uses the Greek demonstrative *ide* and its other form (*idou*) to begin a statement of action or importance. Though the original derivation is from a Greek verb meaning to "see" or "look at," that force was moderated by constant repetition. In this phrase it is not clear whether the sense of the demonstrative is that of actually pointing to the person being mentioned or simply an introduction to the momentous coming of the Messiah, the Lamb of God, the final sacrifice for sin. The title "Lamb of God" is only used twice in the entire Bible, both occurrences being found in the narrative of Jesus' introduction and baptism by John the Baptist (John 1:29, 36). The idea, however, is repeated in 1 Peter 1:19, and the teaching about the Messiah as sacrificial servant is clear from Isaiah 53 and elsewhere.

NASB, NKJV, RSV: Behold, the Lamb of God
NIV: Look, the Lamb of God
LB: Look! (See!) There is the Lamb of God

9
Behold the man (John 19:5)
GREEK: *dou ho anthrōpos*

This short phrase appears only in John 19:5, where it is used by Pontius Pilate to point out the scourged and bleeding Jesus to the crowd. The demonstrative (*idou*) is a derivative of the common verb "to see" and is characteristic in John's gospel, in 1 John, and in the Revelation. The Greek noun *anthrōpos* is the standard term for man as human and masculine. The sense of the phrase is something like "Right there is the man!"

NASB, NKJV, LB: Behold, the Man (man)
NIV, RSV: Here is the man!

10
being justified by faith (Rom. 5:1)
GREEK: *dikaiōthentes . . . ek pisteōs*

This phrase occurs only in Rom. 5:1, although grammatical parallels appear in Rom. 3:26 and Gal. 3:24, contexts that are similar in many emphases. The phrase consists of the nominative present passive participle as the subject, followed by the prepositional phrase (*ek* and its object *pisteōs* in the genitive case).

The concept of the term *justification* is that of a judicial state of men under the wrath, judgment, and curse of God, and needing His pardon (see further Rom. 1:16–3:20, particularly 3:9). Along with that is the assumption that no man can accomplish his own or another's justification (Rom. 3:18-20). The term also assumes that there is no justification found in the works of the law. Although not obtainable by human merit, justification is freely conferred on all who believe. However, it is not an act that originates with man, lest he boast in its results (Rom. 3:27).

In the early chapters of Romans, Paul explains that God justifies the Jews "by faith" (*ek pisteōs*) and the Gentiles "through faith" (another prepositional phrase, *dia tas pisteōs*)—that is, the same kind and condition of faith. In Rom. 5:1 both the justification of Jews and that of Gentiles is covered by the phrase *ek pisteōs*. It envisions the acceptance by God of the believer as righteous. Compare J. Murray, *The Epistle to the Romans* (Grand Rapids: Eerdmans, 1968).

NASB, NKJV: having been justified by faith
NIV: we have been justified through faith
RSV: we are justified by faith
LB: have been made right in God's sight by faith

11
Blessed is the man (Ps. 1:1)
HEBREW: *'ashrê hā'îsh*

This phrase is the opening line of the book of Psalms (1:1). The first psalm in many ways serves as an introduction to the whole collection that follows, and so gives the reader the needed instruction in how to approach that portion of God's Word. The phrase is made up of the masculine plural of a noun meaning "bliss" or "happiness" and the common Hebrew word *'îsh* ("man" or "human"). The term *ashrê* is never used of God's blessing, though it is certainly the result of God's blessing. It appears 26 times in the Psalms and 18 times elsewhere in the Old Testament. The idea of the phrase in Ps. 1:1 is, "Oh the happiness of the man"—the teaching clearly being that there are many happy experiences, in truth a state of bliss, for the man or woman who shuns evil associations and delights in God's Word.

NASB: How blessed is the man
NIV, NKJV, RSV: Blessed is the man
LB: Oh, the joys of those

12
blood and water (John 19:34)
GREEK: *haima kai hudōr*

A short but significant phrase used in John 19:34 to describe the results of the soldier's spear thrust during the crucifixion of Jesus. It is the only description of that event in the gospel narratives. There have been many explanations of this flow from the wound in Jesus' side. The two nouns are common ones: *haima* means "blood" throughout Scripture, and *hudōr* universally means "water." The question is, What does that signify? The answer is found in the nature of crucifixion, which is an agonizing way to bring about asphyxiation. The full weight of the body is suspended from the arms so that insufficient respiration results and the organs slowly die from a loss of oxygen. The immediate result is that the pleural spaces fill with liquid. When the soldier thrust the spear into Jesus' side, the watery fluid from the pleura and the blood from the heart flowed out. That one fact proved beyond any question that Jesus was dead.

All the versions cited read "blood and water."

13
the book of life (Rev. 13:8)
GREEK: *tōi bibliōi tēs zōēs*

The phrase "the book of life" is used in Rev. 13:8; 17:8; 20:12; and 21:27. The Greek *biblion* meant "scroll" throughout the Near East, and a scroll is specifically in view in Rev. 6:14.

The idea of a divine record or list of the righteous is found in the Old Testament as early as Ex. 32:32-33. Such a record is mentioned again in Ps. 69:28 and Dan. 12:1. There is little doubt that the phrase in Revelation is an allusion to the scene in Daniel. It is generally believed that the folio type of book we are familiar with came in with the Christian era and may have even been an innovation of the Christian church. The Bodmer and other early papyrus scraps appear to have come from folio volumes rather than from scrolls.

All the versions cited read "book of life"; some with capitalization.

14
born of water and of the Spirit (John 3:5)
  GREEK: *gennēthēi ex hudatos kai pneumatos*

     Here is another phrase used by Jesus in His discourse with Nicode-
mus (John 3:5). It is introduced with a double *amēn*, usually translated
"Verily, verily," and always used to introduce a statement of unique
importance (see article "Amen"). The phrase consists of words used
again and again in the New Testament. All authorities agree that the
spirit here is indeed the Holy Spirit, but the concept "born of water"
has been variously interpreted. Probably the best approach is to consider what the religious use of water represented in the Old Testament. It
was the great sign and symbol of cleansing (Lev. 1:9, 13; 6:28; 8:6; etc.).
To "be born of water and of the Spirit" is to be cleansed and renewed
by the Holy Spirit.

All the versions cited read "born of water and of the Spirit" (most drop the
second "of").

15
bow ... in the cloud (Gen. 9:14)
  HEBREW: *haqqeshet beʿānān*

     The description of the "bow in the cloud" as a sign of God's covenant
with Noah and his descendants is given at the close of the account of
the Flood (Gen. 9:14). The Hebrew word *qeshet* appears over 70 times in
the Old Testament, usually referring to the archer's bow used both as a
weapon and for killing game (Gen. 27:3). However, it is also used metaphorically for the rainbow in Gen. 9 and in Ezek. 1:28, where it is also
placed in the clouds. Some have proposed that the "bow" was a constellation such as Orion, as in Job 9:9; 38:31; and Amos 5:8, but the context
in Genesis 9 militates against such an interpretation. The verb in Gen.
9:13 is in the past tense, so that the bow was already set before the covenant was made.

  NASB, RSV: bow ... in the cloud(s)
  NIV, LB: rainbow ... in the clouds
  NKJV: rainbow ... in the cloud

16
bush burned with fire (Ex. 3:2)
HEBREW: 'ēsh mittôk hass⁼neh

This phrase is used only in Ex. 3:2, though the event is referred to in Deut. 33:16. The Hebrew term translated "bush" is found nowhere else outside of those two citations. Therefore, though a number of desert shrubs have been proposed as the kind of bush Moses saw, there is no conclusive evidence for any particular one. It is probably a loanword of Egyptian or Midianite origin. The phrase makes clear that the shrub was burning with real flames and that the miraculous event was indicative of the presence of God. The uniqueness of the burning bush reinforced the message of God's presence and Moses' calling as the deliverer of his people.

NASB: the bush was burning with fire
NIV, LB: the bush was on fire
NKJV: the bush burned with fire
RSV: the bush was burning

C

17
called his name (Gen. 4:25)
 HEBREW: *wattiqrā' 'ēt-sh^emô*

Many times this phrase appears in the Old Testament in reference to either men (Gen. 4:25) or women (Gen. 3:20). Both the verb *qārā* and the noun *shēm* are used over 800 times each in various contexts. The verb refers to the specification of a name; in Scripture, as in other Semitic literature, to name a thing was to assert sovereignty or authority over it, as in God's naming of the "day" and the "night" (Gen. 1:5) and Adam's naming of the creatures of the earth (Gen. 2:19).

To name (or call by name) a person not only meant to give him a name but also to indicate either a basic characteristic of the person or, in the case of an infant, an expected characteristic. That is why so many Hebrew names carry with them explanations (or, in effect, etymologies). Such folk etymologies are given for names throughout Semitic literature. But those related meanings often have a far more serious purpose in Scripture—to indicate God's purposes for a person.

The first use of the phrase is in Gen. 3:20 ("And Adam called his wife's name Eve"), to which is added an explanation, a sort of parenthetical statement, "because she was the *mother* of all living" (italics added). The Hebrew for "Eve" is an old Eastern Semite word meaning "mother." Thus it is her career as mother of all living human beings that is the source of her name. The same principle is evident in Gen. 5:29, "And he [Lamech] called his name Noah, saying, 'This same shall comfort us . . . .'" The name "Noah" is derived from a word signifying comfort. Over and over such names are given throughout the Scriptures. The only use of the phrase in its Greek form in the New Testament is in the naming of Jesus (Matt. 1:21).

NASB, NIV, NKJV, LB: named him
RSV: called his name

18
children of Israel (Gen. 32:32)
 HEBREW: *b^enê yiśrā'ēl*

The general term for the nation of Israel throughout the Old Testament. The phrase consists of the Hebrew word for "sons" in a genitive construction with the proper name "Israel" (used first in Gen. 42:5). Because Israel was the name God Himself gave Jacob after the encounter in Gen. 32:28, and because Jacob became the father of twelve sons whose offspring formed the tribes of Israel, the nation could rightly be called the "children of Israel."

The Hebrew word *bēn*, however, does not necessarily indicate biological relationship. Thus the "sons of the prophets" (1 Kings 20:35) means those who followed or were members of the group of the prophets. In time "children of Israel" came to be the common term for "Israelites"— its primary meaning in the over 600 times it is used in the Old Testament.

NASB: sons of Israel
NIV, RSV: the Israelites
NKJV: children of Israel
LB: people of Israel

19
coat of many colours (Gen. 37:3)
   HEBREW: *kᵉtōnet passîm*

This phrase appears in the patriarchal narrative of Israel and Joseph (Gen. 37:3) and in the story of Absalom and his sister Tamar (2 Sam. 13:18-19). The Hebrew term *passîm* occurs only in those two passages, and a variety of meanings have been proposed. The notion that it meant "long sleeves" was popular around the turn of the century. A somewhat similar word has turned up in a cuneiform list, and it is evident that it means a sort of highly ornamented fabric, possibly of Mesopotamian origin. The other word, Hebrew *kᵉtōnet* is a common word for an outer garment (as in Gen. 3:21; Ex. 28:4; and elsewhere). The phrase basically means "an ornamented cloak," which would have indicated a person's social rank in an agricultural society that had distinctive clothing for various occupations and social ranks.

NASB: a varicolored tunic
NIV: a richly ornamented robe
NKJV: a tunic of *many* colors
RSV: a long robe with sleeves
LB: a brightly-colored coat

20

congregation of the saints (Ps. 89:5 [H 6])
  HEBREW: *biqhal qᵉdōshîm*

This second half of the poetic line of Ps. 89:5 is closely related in meaning to the opening line. The psalm is usually considered to be messianic because it celebrates the surety of God's promises.

The phrase contains two fairly common nouns in a genitival relationship. The first noun is the familiar Hebrew term *qāhāl*, which means, "assembly, group, congregation." The word also appears in the Dead Sea Scrolls with the meaning "assembly." However, it is not limited to religious gatherings, but is used of nations (Gen. 35:11), of armies (1 Sam. 17:47), and even of the dead (Prov. 21:16).

The other noun in the phrase is the plural form of the Hebrew *qādôsh*, which refers to anything that is out of the sphere of the ordinary world—that is, something sacred. For that reason it usually means "holy one," and here is where the difficulty enters. The term *holy one* can refer to many different beings in the Old Testament: to God (Ps. 71:22), to pagan temple attendants, probably prostitutes (Deut. 23:17), but more important, to angels (Dan. 4:13, 17, 23). In Ps. 89:5 the term has one of those meanings and does not refer to God's people.

The key to the phrase is the first line of Ps. 89: 5, to which the phrase is parallel. The first line states: "And the heavens shall praise thy wonders, O Lord; thy faithfulness also in the assembly of the holy ones." Since the stars are meant by the metaphor "the heavens shall praise" (in effect, "those that dwell in the heavens"), the parallel must have a similar extraterrestrial reference. As mentioned above, one of the uses of the term *holy ones* is to describe angelic beings. Thus the KJV reading, "congregation of the saints," reflects an unfortunate misunderstanding. It is not until the fifteenth verse that human beings are brought into the forefront of the psalm. The praise of God begins in the heavenly realm.

  NASB, NIV, RSV: assembly of the holy ones
  NKJV: congregation of the saints
  LB: myriads of angels (note: Lit., "the assembly of the holy ones")

21

a convenient season (Acts 24:25)
  GREEK: *kairon*

This familiar phrase, part of Felix's reply to Paul's message about faith in Christ, is simply one word in the original. The term appears a number of times in the New Testament, and its basic meaning is "point of time." In Acts 24:25 it means "time of opportunity." The full meaning of the term is difficult to bring out in English, and there is wide variation in the versions.

NASB: find time
NIV: find it convenient
NKJV: a convenient time
RSV: an opportunity
LB: a more convenient time

22
covenant of salt (Num. 18:19)
HEBREW: *bᵉrît melaḥ*

The phrase is found in Num. 18:19, where it is part of the command to Aaron regarding the funds to be given to the priests forever, in Lev. 2:13 in the reverse order ("the salt of thy covenant"), and in 2 Chron. 13:5, where it is used in the episode of Abijah's attack on Jeroboam and signifies the eternal quality of David's kingdom.

The phrase is straightforward: *bᵉrît*, the noun meaning "covenant," is in construct with the noun *melaḥ* ("salt"), as in Gen. 19:26 and elsewhere, followed by the masculine noun, *ʿôlām* ("forever"). In the ancient world salt was valued for at least three reasons: it was a preservative, an expensive ingredient (it had to be quarried and dried from the Salt Sea or Dead Sea), and a condiment or spice. All three factors would have impressed on the worshipers the importance and permanence of the covenant being made between God and His chosen people.

NASB, NIV: covenant of salt
NKJV, RSV: covenant of salt
LB: permanent contract (note: Literally, "covenant of salt")

23
crown of thorns (Matt. 27:29)
GREEK: *stephanon ex akanthōn*

The crown of thorns put on Jesus' head by the Roman guard is mentioned in three of the gospels (Matt. 27:29; Mark 15:17; John 19:2). The phrase consists of two well-known Greek nouns, the second of which is the object of a prepositional phrase with the preposition *ex* (a form of *ek*) meaning "the substance out of which something is made," as in "man is of the earth" (1 Cor. 15:47) or "clay of the spittle" (John 9:6).

The Greek noun *stephanos* has traditionally been translated "crown." The Latin Vulgate translates it "corona," but the Greek term can also be used for a wreath or other head ornaments. The second noun refers to a common weed with large, very sharp spines. In fact, the Greek term is translated by the Latin Vulgate as "spine." Recent investigations indicate that the "crown of thorns" may have been more of a cap than a wreath of thorns and may have covered, and thereby wounded, the entire top of the head. The best rendering is "a crown out of thorns."

NASB, NIV, NKJV, RSV: crown of thorns
LB: crown from long thorns

24
cunningly devised fables (2 Pet. 1:16)
GREEK: *sesophismenois muthois*

The only occurrence of this phrase is in 2 Pet. 1:16. The unusual perfect passive participle, *sesophismenois,* means "to concoct in a subtle manner." The main noun of the phrase (*muthos*) is "legend, fable," or precisely its cognate in English, "myths," which appears only four other times, each in the pastoral epistles (1 Tim. 1:4; 4:7; 2 Tim. 4:4; Titus 1:14). The phrase is the strongest warning in the whole of the New Testament against legendary or mythological interpretation of the biblical record.

NASB: cleverly devised tales
NIV: cleverly invented stories
NKJV: cunningly devised fables
RSV: cleverly devised myths
LB: fairy tales

D

25

Damsel, I say unto thee, arise (Mark 5:41)
  ARAMAIC: *talitha koum*
  GREEK: *to korasion, soi legō, egeire*

Found only in Mark 5:41, this original Aramaic statement is transliterated in Greek and followed by the Greek translation. The occasion
was the death of the daughter of a synagogue dignitary.

The phrase contains the Aramaic word for "girl" or "little girl" in the
emphatic position and the verb meaning "rise up" in the imperative
mood. It may have been for colloquial reasons that Jesus used what was
ordinarily the masculine form instead of the expected feminine *koumi.*
The occasion argues for the conclusion that Aramaic was the household
language of Jesus' day. His use of it here reveals His tender compassion.
At life's most intimate moments it is common for those who are bilin-
gual to return to their native or childhood tongue.

The Greek is both an interpretation and a translation. The interpretation is found in the words "I say to you" (Greek: *soi legō*). Grammatically, the sentence consists of a noun in the vocative case followed by a
personal pronoun in the dative case, then a present active verb (suggesting continuing present action) in the indicative mood with a present
active imperative verb. Significantly, the Aramaic word *talitha* is rendered *korasion* by Mark. That rather rare Greek word is the diminutive
of *kora* and, therefore, a term of endearment. By using the word Mark
well portrays the emphasis of *talitha.* A *korasion* is a young girl, a little
daughter, who may be barely of marriageable age. Luke renders *talitha*
by the Greek *pais,* meaning simply "child," an accurate but matter-of-
fact translation. Jesus' tenderness toward the young girl may well be a
reflection of the tender love of her father, as revealed in Mark 5:23,
where he calls her his *thugatrion* ("little daughter"). Lest the reader think
she was a very young child, Mark adds that she was twelve years old, a
marriageable age in that culture (5:42). The Greek verb *egeirō* means
"wake up and get up." Jesus' command bore immediate results, and she
arose completely healthy (vv. 42-43).

NASB, NKJV, RSV: Little girl, I say to you, arise

NIV: Little girl, I say to you, get up
LB: Get up, little girl

26
daughter of Belial (1 Sam. 1:16)
HEBREW: *bat-b^eliyyā·al*

Similar phrases appear in Deut. 13:13; Judg. 19:22; 1 Sam. 25:25; 1 Kings 21:13; 2 Chron. 13:7; and Prov. 16:27. The KJV treats the noun *belial* as a proper name. Grammatically, the phrase consists of a noun in construct (*bat*, "daughter") followed by a noun or adjective. In such constructions the terms "daughter(s) of, son(s) of," or "man (men) of" mean "devotee of." The noun *b^eliyyā·al* contains two elements: *b^eli* ("not" or "without") and *yā·al* ("to be of use, worth, or profit"). Hence, a daughter of belial is a useless, worthless, or unprofitable woman. Such individuals may also be base and wicked (Prov. 6:12), plot evil (Prov. 16:27), counsel villainy (Nah. 1:11), and mock justice (Prov. 19:28). In 1 Sam. 1:16 there is the suggestion of evil, insofar as Hannah recognized the impropriety of speaking rather bluntly, if not curtly, to the Lord's priest Eli. That connotation is recognized in most translations.

NASB: a worthless woman
NIV: a wicked woman
NKJV: a wicked woman (note: "daughter of Belial")
RSV: a base woman
LB: just some drunken bum

27
day of our Lord Jesus Christ (1 Cor. 1:8)
GREEK: *en tēi hēmerai tou kuriou hēmōn Iēsou Christou*

This phrase first appears in 1 Cor. 1:8 and reflects Old Testament usage. The similar "day of the Lord" in its eschatological significance occurs frequently in the Old Testament and represents the consummation and comprehensive victory of God's kingdom—a time when His enemies will be punished and His faithful ones rewarded (Joel 2:28, 32).

New Testament use of the phrase often expands the name "Lord" to "Lord Jesus" (1 Cor. 5:5) or "Jesus Christ" (Phil. 1:6), although we also find "day of the Lord" (1 Thess. 5:2; 2 Pet. 3:10) and "day of God" (2 Pet. 3:12). The New Testament writers seem to focus more on the concepts of hope, joy, and victory, but they do not deny the ever-present prediction of judgment on the unrighteous (Rom 2:5-6; 2 Pet. 3:12, etc.). "That day" refers to the same event (Matt. 7:22; 1 Thess. 5:4) as does "the day" (1 Cor. 3:13)—the day Jesus will bodily raise the dead and will reward and glorify believers (Matt. 16:27; John 6:39; Phil. 1:6, 10). That is preeminently the "day of Christ," when His kingdom will be established as an everlasting reign, and sin and death will be forever destroyed (1 Cor. 15).

NASB, NIV, NKJV, RSV: the day of our Lord Jesus Christ
LB: that day when he returns

Nigel Turner, *Christian Words* (Nashville: Nelson, 1981), pp. 138-39.

28
day of the Lord (Isa. 2:12; Acts 2:20)
HEBREW: *yôm yhwh*
GREEK: *hēmeran kuriou*

This phrase first appears in Isa. 2:12, in the prophecy of God's triumph over His enemies and the establishment of His kingdom. The phrase is often connected with "latter days," as in Isa. 2:2 (the beginning of the passage). Most conservative scholars have understood this to be eschatological and point to God's final activity in the era in which the prophet lived.

Some, however, have interpreted the "day of the Lord" to be the end of the Old Testament period and the coming of Christ as the last prophet, priest, and king. But the majority of Bible students understand it to apply to the last judgment, the second coming of Christ, and the consummation of all things. Many apply the term to the establishment of the millennial kingdom.

An often overlooked aspect of the term is that the peoples of antiquity saw themselves as living at the end of a vast period of time. They knew that human history stretched back thousands of years prior to their own day. For them, therefore, it was already the time before the end, the long-awaited "day of the Lord." The phrase is used in Joel 2:31, which is in turn quoted by Peter in his sermon on the day of Pentecost (Acts 2:20). It is clear from the Dead Sea Scrolls that eschatology was in the forefront of the Jewish interpretation of that time. All those facts are certainly related to the time of Christ's advent in that very age.

NASB: Lord of hosts will have a day / day of the Lord
NIV: The Lord Almighty has a day / day of the Lord

NKJV: day of the Lord of hosts / day of the Lord
RSV: the Lord of hosts has a day / day of the Lord
LB: On that day the Lord of Hosts / Day of the Lord

29
dove's dung (2 Kings 6:25)
HEBREW: *hireyyônîm*

This phrase is found only in a difficult passage in 2 Kings 6:25, in the narrative of a siege of Samaria by the Aramaean king Ben-Hadad II, around 850 B.C. It is used to describe the desperate plight of the inhabitants, who were starving within the walled city and faced certain and cruel death if they tried to escape. The episode is told as part of the story of the prophet Elisha. The phrase illustrates the terrible inflation in food prices brought about by the siege: "And there was a great famine in Samaria; and, behold, they besieged it, until an ass's head was sold for fourscore pieces of silver, and the fourth part of a cab of dove's dung for five pieces of silver."

Since under no circumstances could human life be sustained by the eating of bird droppings, this strange and unique phrase must refer to some other substance, which was not usually used as food but which could be eaten. The ancient rabbinical commentators were so taken back by the apparent horror of the text that they proposed numerous emendations. Evidence from the context suggests that the term refers to a plant that was used for food only as a last resort.

Plant names appear with some frequency in ancient, nonbiblical texts and are often similar to modern common plant names in being a combination of fanciful usage and tradition (as our "fox glove" and "lady's slipper"). None of those words has any actual relationship to the plant denoted, but such names are widely used. Some possible plants suggested include a species of wild onion and various Arabic terms involving "bird's milk" or "bird's dung," the common name of the plant known in English as "Star of Bethlehem," which is said to be edible when boiled or roasted.

But there are two serious problems with fitting such explanations into the other elements of the story. The other commodity mentioned as being sold at an exorbitant price and equally unfit for human food is an "ass's head." In the verses following 2 Kings 6:25, there is a particularly grisly story about an argument between two women who had boiled and eaten the one woman's son and were subsequently contending over the fate of the second woman's son. In the light of that event, the dove's dung cannot have been a substance either desirable or palatable for human food in any way. If eaten at all, it must have been consumed by animals or persons only in the most desperate of straits.

A second problem is the measure mentioned in the text along with dove's dung. The word *qab* occurs only in this passage and is known to be a dry measure. Josephus, the Jewish historian of the first century A.D., considered it to be equal to a Roman measure for dry quantities of vegetables and grains—probably less than a quart. A fourth part of a *qab*, therefore, was little more than a handful. A dictionary or lexical text from the Kassite period of Babylonian-Assyrian history gives the exact linguistic equivalent of the phrase in 2 Kings 6:25. From the dry measure and the lexical text it is apparent that dove's dung was a common and perhaps slang term for the carob pod, the tough fibrous seed case of the locust tree that has been used as animal fodder in the Near East for centuries. The use of carob pods as food by the lowest classes is mentioned from another Babylonian source. A cuneiform text entitled *The Theodicy* contains a statement about the hardships visited upon a certain individual.

As the noble and the rich (who have now fallen into poverty),
The carob pod is now their food.

It is clear that 2 Kings 6:25 seeks to convey the message that the once proud people of Samaria had been reduced by the severity of the famine to paying an outrageous price for a meager handful of feed only marginally fit for animals. The primary point of the story, however, is to celebrate redemption by the Lord, as told by the prophet Elisha in the king's presence. In judgment on their rebellion, God caused the inhabitants of Samaria, who were accustomed to the finest of foods and the choicest of drinks, to be so impoverished by a foreign and heathen power that they became less than beggars.

Even the Palestinian Talmud, a repository of the wisdom of the oriental rabbis, states that carob pods were the food of animals. It seems to have been part of the folk wisdom of the ancient Near East. The biblical use of it to teach that disobedience to God can bring down a curse in the form of such want and poverty that humans will long for animal food appears again in Jesus' parable of the prodigal son: "And he went and joined himself to a citizen of that country; and he sent him into his fields to feed swine. And he would fain have filled his belly with the [carobs] that the swine did eat: and no man gave unto him. And when he came to himself, he said, How many hired servants of my father's have bread enough and to spare, and I perish with hunger!" (Luke 15:15-18).

NASB, RSV, LB: dove's dung

NIV: seed pods (note: Or "dove's dung")
NKJV: dove droppings

M. Held, "Studies in Comparative Semitic Lexicography," in *Studies for B. Landsberger* (Chicago: U. of Chicago Press, 1965), pp. 395-98.

30
drew a bow at a venture (1 Kings 22:34)
HEBREW: *māshak baqqeshet l^etūmô*

Found only in 1 Kings 22:34 and its parallel 2 Chron. 18:33, this phrase consists of a verb in the base stem followed by a prepositional phrase, plus the adverbial phrase (literally, "in his guilelessness"). This use of the Hebrew *māshak* ("drawing") is rare, although the verb does picture the action of pulling or drawing someone or something toward a goal. The verb is used elliptically, denoting the complete act of drawing the bowstring back, releasing it, and letting the arrow fly. The archer aimed at the enemy in general and not at any specific target; he intended to hit someone, but not a particular soldier.

In this context this is a most intriguing statement. Through the mouth of the prophet Micaiah God had told King Ahab that He had sent a lying spirit into the mouth of the false prophets, a spirit that God said would entice Ahab. The spirit would not simply tempt Ahab but would convince him to enter the battle. To try to forestall his death, prophesied by Micaiah, Ahab disguised himself as an ordinary soldier. But his disguise was to no avail. God's prophecy came true, even though the enemy soldier who shot the arrow had no idea he would hit King Ahab.

NASB, NIV: drew his bow at random
NKJV: drew a bow at random
RSV: drew his bow at a venture
LB: shot an arrow at random

E

31
elders of Israel (Ex. 3:18)
   HEBREW: *ziqnê yiśrā'ēl*

This phrase consists of a plural noun in construct followed by a noun in the absolute. "Elder" is used in its technical sense over 100 times in the Old Testament. The term *ziqnê* means "bearded" and by extension an older male, or elder. It first occurs in Ex. 3:18, where Moses is commanded to take the elders of Israel with him before Pharaoh. Those elders were probably heads over clans, the extended families including brothers, cousins, children, other relatives, and their families.

Later, "elder" was used of judges whose positions were attained by virtue of election rather than merely being the oldest male in a clan. Those elder-judges sat at city gates adjudicating all cases (see Ex. 18:13-16; Deut. 17:8-13; 19:12; 21:2, 19; 22:15; Ruth 4:9, 11). The elders were appointed over thousands, hundreds, fifties, and tens (of families, Deut. 1:15). Consequently, they were organized into layers of courts, with a supreme judge over all (Deut. 17:8-9). Also, there were two parallel court systems, one dealing with civil matters and the other with ecclesiastical affairs. The New Testament attests the continuation of that system in the existence of the Sanhedrin (Mark 15:55; Luke 22:66; Acts 5: 27, 34, 41; etc.) and to some extext in the early church (Acts 11:30; 14:23; 15:1-35; 1 Tim. 3; Titus 1; etc.).

NASB, NIV, NKJV, RSV: elders of Israel
LB: elders of the people of Israel

32
Elect according to the foreknowledge of God (1 Pet. 1:2)
   GREEK: *eklektois . . . kata prognōsin theou*

This phrase, found only in 1 Pet. 1:2 (the Greek includes part of verse 1), consists of a noun in the dative case (as the indirect object) and a prepositional phrase. A noun preceded by a preposition is usually definite; hence, "according to *the* foreknowledge." Peter addresses himself to the Christians whom he identifies as being "elect" or "chosen." With that identification he recognizes that out of all mankind God has selected them to be His very own. God's election occurred before the foundation of the world (Eph. 1:4) and was not based on any merit in those whom He elected.

The prepositional phrase strengthens that idea. They were elect according to, or by virtue of, the divine foreknowledge, which specifies the origin of their election. Because God foreknew them He elected or chose them. Jesus was handed over by the predetermined plan of God (Acts 2:23), and consequently it was foreknown by Him. Thus God's foreknowledge involves more than simple prescience. So Paul can argue in Rom. 11:2 that God has not rejected His people whom He foreknew. Those whom God foreknew He predestined to be redeemed (Rom. 8:28-29).

NASB, NIV: chosen according to the foreknowledge of God
NKJV: elect according to the foreknowledge of God
RSV: chosen and destined by God
LB: chose you long ago and knew you would become his children

Nigel Turner, *Christian Words* (Nashville: Nelson, 1981), pp. 127-30.

33
Enoch ... prophesied (Jude 14)
GREEK: *eprophēteusen ... Henōch*

A strange phrase found only in Jude 14. The words are well known, and the grammar is not complex.

The question it raises is, Where did Enoch prophesy? There is certainly no such quotation or incident in the Old Testament. A Book of Enoch is contained in the collection of the pseudepigrapha ("false writings"). This book existed in Ethiopic and Greek for centuries, and an Aramaic version was discovered among the Dead Sea Scrolls. But there is no statement in the book corresponding exactly to the reference in Jude. However, the general themes of the Book of Enoch that involve visions of the future history of Israel and declarations of judgment are certainly closely related to a number of passages in the New Testament.

NASB, NIV, NKJV, RSV: Enoch ... prophesied
LB: Enoch ... knew about these men and said this

34

enquired and searched diligently (1 Pet. 1:10)

    GREEK: *exezētēsan kai exēreunēsan*

Only in 1 Pet. 1:10. The two verbs in the aorist active indicative point to the past inquiring and searching by God's prophets. As the LB paraphrases, "They had many questions as to what it all could mean." Prophets of Peter's day no longer needed to inquire and search the way their predecessors had, for now the Person and time of the consummation of salvation had been revealed and was known (1 Pet. 1:11). Now there was no frustration in not knowing those matters clearly (v. 12). The verbs are made more emphatic by the addition of the prepositional prefix *ex* (a form of *ek*). To indicate that strengthening, translators have added such words as "diligently," "careful," and "intently."

    NASB: made careful search and inquiry
    NIV: searched intently and with the greatest care
    NKJV: inquired and searched diligently
    RSV: searched and inquired
    LB: they had many questions as to what it all could mean

35

entertained angels unawares (Heb. 13:2)

    GREEK: *elathon tines xenisantes aggelous*

The full phrase, "for thereby some have entertained angels unawares," appears only in Heb. 13:2. It is appended as a sort of summary of proof texts to an exhortation to Christian hospitality, and refers to such incidents as Abraham's entertainment of the three angels on their way to judge and destroy Sodom (Gen. 18) and Lot's reception of them (Gen. 19).

The phrase contains the aorist tense of the common Greek verb *lanthanō* ("to escape notice"), which occurs six times in the New Testament. In Mark 7:24; Luke 8:47; and Acts 26:26 it means "to be hidden"; and in two places (2 Pet. 3:5, 8) it means "to be ignorant of." Only in Heb. 13:2 does it mean "unawares," that is, "without realization." The other major component of the phrase is the participle of the verb *xenizō* ("to entertain"), as seen in Acts 10:6, 18, 23, 32; 21:16; 28:7; etc. The usage is typically Greek in that the notion of entertainment is put into participial form and attached to what is really the direct object of the verb, "to be unawares."

NASB, NIV: entertained angels without knowing it
NKJV: unwittingly entertained angels
RSV: entertained angels unawares
LB: entertained angels without realizing it

36
even to the dividing asunder of soul and spirit, and of the joints and marrow (Heb. 4:12)

GREEK: *diiknoumenos archi merismou psuchēs kai pneumatos, harmōn te kai muelōn*

Occurs only in Heb. 4:12, as do the words *harmōn* ("joints") and *muelōn* ("marrow"). Actually, the phrase is the object of the preposition *archi* ("to," "up to"). The entire prepositional phrase modifies the participle *diikoumenos* ("piercing" or "penetrating"). The phrase opens with a noun of action, *merismou* (in the genitive case), which is modified by four other nouns, each in the genitive case. Those four nouns form two pairs, each element in the pair being joined by *kai* ("and").

The interpretation of this phrase has caused considerable debate. Some understand it to mean "division of the soul from the spirit, and division of the joints from the marrow." Grammatically, however, (because of the *te*; compare Luke 24:30; Acts 26:30) it is better understood to mean "division of the soul and spirit" (the immaterial aspects of man) from "the joints and marrow" (man's material side). It would be well not to build too much on the distinction between soul and spirit, inasmuch as no such distinction appears in the creation account (Gen. 1–2), in the intermediate state of the dead (Eccles. 12:7; Phil. 1:23), or in the union of the material and immaterial parts of man in the resurrection (1 Thess. 5:23). It is noteworthy that the word *marrow* is used. The passage clearly teaches that the Word of God unveils man's deepest nature, inmost thoughts, and secret inclinations.

NASB: as far as the division of soul and spirit, of both joints and marrow
NIV: even to dividing soul and spirit, joints and marrow
NKJV: even to the division of soul and spirit, and of joints and marrow
RSV: to the division of soul and spirit, of joints and marrow
LB: our innermost thoughts and desires with all their parts

37
eyes of the Lord (Gen. 6:8)

HEBREW: *bᵉ῾ênê yhwh*

A frequently occurring phrase that first appears in Gen. 6:8. In form it is a prepositional phrase appended to the dual noun *'ênayim* ("eyes") in the construct state, followed by the divine name (the tetragrammaton, YHWH). Here is the convenantal name for God. Known by that name long before Moses (see Gen. 4:1), God added a special dimension to the name in Moses' day. The Lord was the one who not only gave the covenant but who also kept it (Ex. 6:3). That marked the beginning of the fulfillment of His covenant to lead His people into the Promised Land.

God is a spirit and does not have a body like men (Deut. 4:15-18; John 4:24). Therefore, when the Bible attributes bodily parts to God, it is speaking metaphorically and anthropomorphically—that is, as if God had a body as men do. So the "eyes of the Lord" represent His observing presence, His opinion or judgment, His mind or consciousness, and His active presence.

As a figure of His presence, His eyes are everywhere, observing good and evil (Prov. 15:3). He observes such matters not just externally but inwardly, so as to see the intent of the thoughts of the heart (Gen. 6:5) and man's very nature (Gen. 8:21). God's eyes are not only vehicles through which He gains information, but are directly linked to the exercise of His judgment or opinion. So, to do or be evil or good in God's eyes is to do or be good or evil in God's judgment, to please or displease Him (Gen. 38:7; Lev. 10:19; Deut. 4:25; 6:18).

Eyes may also represent mind or consciousness. Noah found favor in God's eyes (Gen. 6:8). Jacob, knowing he deserved Esau's wrath and that Esau was in a position to do him great harm, asked that he might find favor (grace) in his brother's eyes. He asked that Esau be favorably disposed toward him—that they be reconciled.

Finally, God's eyes symbolize His active presence, effecting His will in behalf of the righteous (2 Chron. 16:9) and against the wicked (Amos 9:8). Consequently, if His eyes are closed, man is shut off and prayers go unanswered (2 Kings 19:16; Isa. 1:15). On the other hand, if His eyes are open to men, He sustains and delivers them (Pss. 33:18; 34:15).

All the versions cited read "eyes of the Lord," except the LB, which reads "Noah was a pleasure to the Lord."

F

38
upon the face of the deep (Gen. 1:2)
HEBREW: ʿal-pᵉnê tᵉhôm

The first and primary occurrence of this phrase is in Gen. 1:2. The phrase begins with the preposition ʿal, functioning in its primary signification of "upon" or "over." Next comes the plural noun pᵉnê, here appearing in the construct and meaning "surface" (its primary connotation being "face"). The noun tᵉhôm is a Semitic word signifying a large body of water. In the Hebrew Bible it refers not only to the primordial waters covering the entire global surface (Gen. 1:2), but to the Red Sea (Isa. 51:10), the Mediterranean Sea (Jonah 2:5), and deep fresh-water-producing springs (Ps. 78:15; Ezek. 31:4). The phrase occurs only one other place in the Bible (Prov. 8:27), although a near equivalent is in Job 38:30.

Some scholars have tried to argue that the Bible sets forth an erroneous cosmology, including a subterranean ocean that is organically connected with the salt water oceans. That analysis, however, completely ignores the extraordinary factual accuracy of passages such as Job 26:7. Older exegetes have linked the Hebrew tᵉhôm to the Akkadian word Tiʾamat, the name of the Mesopotamian salt water goddess. From that they deduced a conceptual relationship between the Akkadian creation story called Enuma Elish and Genesis 1. They charged that Genesis 1 was a reworked version of the Enuma Elish. More recent scholarship, however, has demonstrated that such an approach is etymologically unsound. Most modern scholars reject the supposed linguistic connection and, in fact, tᵉhôm appears to be an earlier form than the Akkadian name.

NASB, NIV: surface of the deep
NKJV: on the face of the deep
RSV: upon the face of the deep
LB: over the dark vapors

W. White, Jr.,"*The Seven Tablets of Creation,*" Master's thesis, Westminster Theological Seminary, 1963.

39

face of the Lord (Ps. 34:16 [H v. 17])
   HEBREW: *pᵉnê yhwh*

A primary passage displaying the meaning of this phrase is Ps. 34:16. The phrase consists of a plural noun in the construct state followed by a noun in the absolute.

The divine name *YHWH* consists of the four Hebrew letters for God's covenantal name (the tetragrammaton), with the vowels of the Hebrew word *'ădōnāy* ("lord") inserted, because pious Jews refused to pronounce the divine name. Instead they read *'ădōnāy*. The name YHWH, sometimes translated "Yahweh" or "Jehovah," focuses uniquely on God as the giver (Gen. 4:1) and keeper (Ex. 6:3) of the covenant.

Since God is pure spirit (John 4:24), He has no bodily parts (Deut. 4:15-18). Therefore, the references to His face are metaphorical and anthropomorphical, that is, they ascribe to God human bodily attributes for teaching purposes. This phrase represents the presence and person of God. To see Him face-to-face is to be in His immediate presence. The Jews distinguished between appearing before God's face in the sense of formal worship (Ex. 23:15; 34:20) and actually looking upon His person, that is, His holiness. The former was expressed by a special infinitive form plus the word for face (Hebrew *lirᵒōt pānāy*). To actually gaze on God, however, was impossible to do and still live (Ex. 33:20). Yet it was possible to see the angel of the Lord face to face (or, as many believe, the Lord Jesus in a preincarnate form, Gen. 32:30; Judg. 6:22).

God's face also represents His person, so that His face indicates His disposition. His face may fall in anger or displeasure (Jer. 3:12). It may be hidden in aversion or disgust (Ps. 13:1). One can cause God's face to become sweet, that is, conciliate Him or seek His favor (1 Kings 13:6). The turning away of God's face indicates His displeasure (Ps. 34:16), even as its turning toward someone connotes His compassion and concern (2 Chron. 30:9).

NASB, NIV, NKJV, RSV: face of the Lord
LB: the Lord has made up his mind

40

And that because of **false brethren unawares brought in** (Gal. 2:4)
   GREEK: *dia de tous pareisaktous pseudadelphous*

A prepositional phrase found in Gal. 2:4. It is introduced by the preposition *dia* ("on account of, because of"), the object of which is *pseudadelphous,* itself modified by the adjective *pareisaktous.* The particle *de* serves to heighten the force of the phrase and should be rendered "but." The definite article *tous* shows that the false brethren possibly were known to Paul's original readers.

The adjective appears only here in the Bible, being what is known as a hapax legomenon (a word used only once). Extrabiblical sources teach that *pareisaktous* means "brought in," and that it often bears overtones of secret and malicious subversion. The noun *pseudadelphous* consists of two elements well known in Greek vocabulary: *pseudo* ("false") and *adelphous* ("brethren"). The combined form appears one other time in the New Testament (2 Cor. 11:26).

In Galatians the apostle is referring to those who came to the church as brothers but were not true believers. They were members of the organized church but not members of the true, spiritual church. They professed Christ but did not possess His salvation. Paul knew that only because of such pretenders was the suggestion made that Titus be circumcised. They had sneaked in to spy out and destroy the church's freedom from bondage to the Jewish law, but their perversity was exposed.

NASB: false brethren who had sneaked in
NIV: false brothers had infiltrated our ranks
RSV, NKJV: false brethren secretly brought in
LB: some so-called "Christians" there—false ones, really—who came to spy

41
feast of the dedication (John 10:22)
GREEK: *ta egkainia*

This phrase, a hapax legomenon, occurs only in John 10:22. John's readers were well familiar with this feast. Indeed, beginning about the twenty-fifth of Kislev (roughly our Dec. 25) 165 B.C., when Judas Maccabaeus rededicated the Temple in Jerusalem, the feast had been observed annually. Celebrated for eight days, it was a joyous occasion, involving the lighting of homes and, for many, a trip to Jerusalem. It was the rainy season in Jerusalem, so it is not surprising to find Jesus walking in the Temple complex under the portico called Solomon's, reputedly the only portion of the earlier Temple remaining after Nebuchadnezzar's invasion. The feast is known by several names: "Hanukkah," "the feast of dedication," "the feast of lights."

NASB: Feast of the Dedication

NIV: Feast of Dedication
NKJV: the Feast of Dedication
RSV: the feast of the Dedication
LB: the Dedication Celebration

Nigel Turner, *Christian Words* (Nashville: Nelson, 1981), p. 104.

42
feast of unleavened bread (Luke 22:1)
GREEK: *hē heortē tōn azumōn*

The full phrase occurs only in Luke 22:1, although the word *azumōn*, referring to the feast, appears in Matt. 26:17; Mark 14:1, 12; Luke 22:7; and Acts 12:3; 20:6. Grammatically the phrase consists of the definite article, the noun "feast," and a second noun with the definite article. The plural form of the final noun may be explained as a reference to the many cakes of bread consumed during that season, somewhat similar to the Hebrew name for the feast, *maṣṣôt*, a plural form.

The feast lasted for seven days following the celebration of Passover, from the fifteenth to the twenty-first of Nisan. It commemorated the early days of Israel's wilderness journeys, during which only unleavened bread was eaten (Ex. 12:14-20). According to the custom of Jesus' day, unleavened bread had to be eaten at the Passover, which was held the first night of the feast of unleavened bread (Mark 14:1, 12; Luke 22:7, cf. Ex. 12:15, 18, etc.). During the rest of the week it was not mandatory to eat bread, but all bread eaten had to be unleavened or the offender was cast out of the Temple (Ex. 12:15, 19; 13:3; Deut. 16:3).

Every day of the week saw multiple and varied offerings, while the first (Passover proper) and seventh days were days of holy convocation. On those days all labor except what was necessary was forbidden, and the pious were summoned to special offerings and other acts of worship. On Monday of that week the barley harvest was dedicated to the Lord. The feast was observed during our months of March and April. As Luke 22:1 states, the entire period of the feast of Unleavened Bread was known as the Passover.

NASB, NIV, NKJV: the Feast of Unleavened Bread
RSV: the feast of Unleavened Bread
LB: the Passover celebration

43
firmament in the midst (Gen. 1:6)
 HEBREW: *rāqîaʿ bᵉtôk*

This phrase occurs in the first few verses of the narrative of creation (Gen. 1:6). Neither Hebrew term in the phrase is common in the Old Testament. The noun *rāqîaʿ* basically developed from the notion of "stamping out" or "spreading out." One derivation refers to a covering or the space existing over something. It is the last meaning that is used in Gen. 1:6. The same term appears in 1:20—"let birds fly above the earth across the expanse [*rāqîaʿ*] of heaven" (NIV).

The KJV reading, "firmament," is particularly unfortunate, though easily explained. Many ancient Near Eastern cultures thought of the heavens as being a concave curved surface—a hard, possibly metallic or stone vault. The terms for those ideas made their way into usage in the various cultures for centuries thereafter. From Egyptian usage, probably in Alexandria, the idea of a vault made of hard material was introduced into the Septuagint translation of the Old Testament with the Greek word *stereōma* ("the solid part"). That term was in turn translated into the Latin *firmamentum* in the Vulgate and from there into English. The KJV reading is therefore clearly misleading. The best possible translation is "an open expanse in the midst," or "an expanse in the midst."

NASB: an expanse in the midst
NIV: an expanse between the waters
NKJV, RSV: a firmament in the midst
LB: Let the vapors separate (note: Lit., "Let there be a dome to divide the waters.")

44
firstborn of every creature (Col 1:15)
 GREEK: *prōtotokos pasēs ktiseōs*

This phrase occurs only in Col. 1:15. It consists of the noun *prōtotokos* modified by the noun *ktiseōs* (genitive case), which in turn is modified by the adjective *pasēs*. *Ktisis* ("creature") occurs frequently in the New Testament and refers either to the act of creation or to the thing created, whether individual things or the creation as a whole. Here the grammar limits its meaning to individual created beings, for it would have been preceded by the definite article were it to refer to the creation as a whole.

Thus the noun and its adjective appear in the genitive of comparison—that is, Christ is firstborn in comparison to every other creature. Verse 16 makes abundantly clear that there is not the slightest suggestion here that Christ is a created being, a truth further supported by the phrase "the image of the invisible God." The latter statement identifies Christ's essential nature as divine and, therefore, not part of the creation.

The word *prōtotokos* also focuses on the divine nature of Christ and does not merely make an identification. It relates to His origin and position and speaks of the means and time of His origin. Distinct from the *ktiseis* ("created ones"), Christ is born of God (*tokos*). They are creatures; He is uncreated. He is eternally begotten of God. The eternal begetting temporally preceded the creation, so that He is the "firstborn." The idea of the firstborn is well known in the Old Testament. God's firstborn is the heir and ruler of all things (Ex. 4:22; Ps. 89:27; Jer. 31:9; cf. Heb. 1:1-2). The phrase proves Jesus Christ to be prior to, distinct from, and highly exalted over every created person and thing.

NASB: the first-born of all creation
NIV, NKJV: the firstborn over all creation
RSV: the first-born of all creation
LB: He existed before God made anything at all

45
For three ... and for four (Prov. 30:21)
HEBREW: *taḥat shālôsh ... wᵉ taḥat ʼarbaʻ*

This phrase occurs in Prov. 30:21, although a phrase bearing similar significance first appears in Ex. 20:5. It consists of the cardinal numbers three and four, each preceded by the preposition signifying "unto" and joined by a conjunction. This was a familiar poetic device in ancient Semitic literature. In Babylonian, the "hymnal-epic dialect" raised it to a high art. The standard was to have eight elements balanced in A and B clauses. The epic would set in contrast a series: statement 1 ... then statement 2; statement 3 ... then statement 4 (the form in the Proverbs passage); statement 5 ... then statement 6; statement 7 ... then a new subject or dramatic change of direction in the drama introduced as statement 8. There is a definite pattern of this sort in the narrative of creation in Genesis, and the seventh day, seventh week, and seventieth week-year are used throughout Scripture. The world was created in seven days, Christ arose the first day after the seven-day week, and so on.

Such phrases are typical of a whole series of similar phrases formally consisting of a number (x) in the A position and $x + 1$ in the B position.

In a few cases such a series represents an arithmetic value, with the *B* character being determinative—as in Prov. 30:21, where four things are listed after the phrase. In most instances, however, the indication is poetic rather than arithmetic. In other words, it represents an indeterminate small number. Thus, in Amos 1:3 it is the few (but weighty and heinous) sins of Damascus that summon God's judgment. That understanding is especially important in interpreting passages such as Ex. 20:5. God will visit one's iniquity upon his descendants. He will also reward righteousness with a long period of blessing upon one's descendants.

NASB, NIV, RSV: Under three things . . . under four
NKJV: For three *things* . . . Yes, for four
LB: There are three things . . . no, four

W. White, Jr., 'Number,' in M.C. Tenney, ed., *The Zondervan Pictorial Encyclopedia of the Bible* (Grand Rapids: Zondervan, 1975), 4:452-61.

46
four corners of the earth (Isa. 11:12)
HEBREW: *mĕ'arba' kan^epôt hā'āreṣ*

This phrase occurs only twice in the Old Testament, both times in poetic contexts (Isa. 11:12; Ezek. 7:2). There are three words in the original, an adjective and two nouns. The first word is the common Hebrew word for "four," and the primary noun is the Hebrew word usually meaning "wing," as of a bird, but also meaning "hem" or "skirt," actually the "edge" of a robe (as in 1 Sam. 15:27). The confusion over the extensions of the meaning resulted in the KJV's translating the word (*kānāp*) as "wing" 70 times, as "skirt" 14 times, as "border, corner, end," and "feathered" twice each, and also as "overspreading, quarter, uttermost part, flying, other, sort, winged." Obviously most of those ideas are incorrect.

The phrase is not unusual in other Semitic texts, and phrases with similar meanings, such as "four quarters" or "four shores" of the earth, can be found as early as 2000 B.C. That is the idea foremost here. The best rendering is "the four regions of the earth," meaning the extremes in each of the four directions.

NASB, NKJV, RSV: the four corners of the earth
NIV: the four quarters of the earth
LB: the ends of the earth; east, west, north or south

G

Galilee of the Gentiles (Matt. 4:15)
  GREEK: *Galilaia tōn ethnōn*

This phrase, in Hebrew, also occurs in Isa. 9:1. The Greek consists of a noun modified by a plural noun in the genitive. The modifying noun is made definite by the preceding definite article (*tōn*). *Galilee* is a Greek transliteration of the Hebrew word, whose root meaning is "circuit" or "district." The area involved is about 60 miles long and 30 miles wide including the Lake or Sea of Galilee. It consists of varied terrain, including high hills and very fertile plains. Fairly well watered, it may be described as cool, lush, and picturesque. Within this district were the cities of Kadesh (a city of refuge), Chorazin, Bethshan, Megiddo, Cana, Nain, Nazareth, and Capernaum.

The modern capital and trading center is Tiberias, originally built by the Romans. This territory was originally assigned to the tribes of Asher, Naphtali, Issachar, and Zebulun, but was never fully possessed. Its population was a mixture of Jews and heathen Gentiles. Isaiah, therefore, referred to it as "Galilee of the Gentiles."

The racial mixture was increased when Judas Maccabaeus forced all the inhabitants of the region to become Jews. Galilean Jews were intensely patriotic and religious even though held in contempt by the pure-blooded Jews of Judea and Jerusalem (John 1:46; 7:52). Several well-known Old Testament figures—Barak, Gideon, Ibzan, Elon, Tola, Jonah, Elijah, and perhaps Hosea—came from Galilee. Jesus, too, came from Galilee (although He was born in Bethlehem), as did eleven of the twelve apostles. Much of His public ministry also occurred there.

NASB, NIV, NKJV, RSV: Galilee of the Gentiles (NASB note: Or, "nations")
LB: Upper Galilee where so many foreigners live

garden of Eden (Gen. 2:15)
  HEBREW: *gan-ʿēden*

The first occurrence of this phrase is in Gen. 2:15, but it appears in Gen. 3:23-24; Ezek. 36:35; and Joel 2:3. The word *eden* alone is in Gen. 2:8, 10; 4:16; Isa. 51:3; Ezek. 28:13; 31:9, 16, 18. *Gan* simply means "garden," and *'ēden* is a proper name transliterated in English as "Eden." The Garden of Eden is perhaps the best known garden in literature, and may have been located near the mouth of the Persian Gulf. There is some evidence that a "garden of Eden" was a subject of some very ancient pre-Hebraic poems and epics. A detailed but very difficult reference is found in Ezek. 31:8-18.

Eden was specifically designed by God to be the perfect home for mankind, but due to the sin of Adam and Eve, they were driven from the garden. In fact God placed angels at its portals to prevent man from returning (Gen. 3). From that time on mankind has longed to return to Eden, has been barred from it, and yet is promised Eden regained and renewed through God's covenant.

Later called the "garden of the Lord," Eden served as a symbol of fertile, prosperous land (Gen. 13:10; Isa. 51:3; Ezek. 36:35; Joel 2:3). In Ezek. 31:8-18 the garden of God appears to be the world, with its trees being the "kings" of the world.

The beauty of Eden—where there was no sin, no animosity between the earth's creatures, no want, and no death—became a symbol of blessing throughout biblical history. Palestine became a type of Eden, the land of rest (Deut. 12:9; 1 Kings 8:56), where there would be no poor or oppressed (Deut. 15:4), no hunger, no barrenness of man or beast, no sickness, and no enemies (Deut. 7:12-16)—if the people would obey the Lord. The blessings become unconditional when the prophets speak of the messianic age (Isa. 32:1-8; 41:17; 58:7-8; 61:1-11). Jesus spoke in terms of fulfilling the promise of Eden perfected (Matt. 9:35; 10:7; 11:4-5, 29; cf. Isa. 11:4-11; Ezek. 36:30, 35), whose full realization would come only after His second coming (Heb. 4; Rev. 22:1-3). The New Testament also speaks of perfected Eden as the paradise of eternity (Luke 23:43; 2 Cor. 12:3-4; Rev. 2:7).

All the versions cited read "Garden (garden) of Eden"

U. Cassuto, *A Commentary on the Book of Genesis* (Jerusalem: Hebrew U. Press, 1961), pp. 71-83.

49
Glory to God in the highest (Luke 2:14)
  GREEK: *doxa en hupsistois theōi*

This clause appears only in Luke 2:14 and consists of the noun *doxa* ("glory"), the preposition *en*, the word *hupsistois* (the superlative of the adverb *hupsi*) used here as a substantive, and the direct object, the noun *theos* ("God"). The meaning of the clause *en hupsistois* is evident from the structure of the angelic announcement. Being parallel to "on earth," it is clearly a location. It does not refer simply to the heavens as that region in the cosmos corresponding to earth, so that God's glory is manifest in the entire cosmos. Rather it refers to God's dwelling place (perhaps, "highest heaven"). In Luke 19:38 the crowds shout, "Peace in heaven, and glory in the highest" (cf. Matt. 21:9).

The meaning of "glory" is tied to the syntactical structure of the angel's statement. Since "peace on earth" is not a wish but a declaration of the significance of Jesus' birth among men with whom God is pleased, the word *glory*, being syntactically parallel, is a declaration of affairs in heaven. The Prince of Peace has come, He whose government and peace shall know no end (Isa. 9:6-7); the salvation of God is here and the message of peace is being joyfully declared (Isa. 52:7-10). Christ's birth was a manifestation of God's glory in heaven. In Luke 2:14, therefore, glory refers to the divine attribute whose fullness God Himself already possessed, but which has been made manifest by the birth of the Savior. God's glory, grace, and peace rest upon everyone who truly does good (Rom. 2:10). It is the God of all peace who has established salvation for His people, and to Him all glory belongs (Heb. 13:20-21; 1 Pet. 4:11).

NASB, NIV, NKJV, RSV: Glory to God in the highest
LB: Glory to God in the highest heaven

50

And **God said** (Gen. 1:3)
   HEBREW: *wayyō 'mēr 'ĕlōhîm*

This frequently occurring phrase is first used in Gen. 1:3 and consists of the verb *'āmar* followed by the divine title *'Ĕlōhîm*. The attached conjunctive (*wa*) introduces God's actions once He has already set the stage, and it is properly rendered "then." *'Ĕlōhîm*, in the plural of majesty, is well suited to embrace the unity and yet plurality of the true God (Gen. 1:2, 26). In the Bible *'Ĕlōhîm* is the only true God, and this name focuses on Him as sovereign over all (Deut. 10:17). This universally sovereign One is the Savior-God of His people (Gen. 17:8; Ps. 18:46).

Though *'āmar* simply means "to say," the sovereign God's speaking bears the force of the divine, sovereign will. If He says something with the intention and will that it will be accomplished, it comes to be. In Gen. 1:3, therefore, because "and God said" constitutes an announcement of His sovereign will, what is announced immediately occurs. The sovereign God's "saying" is also revelatory. By "saying" to men God reveals to them His will (Lev. 12:1-2). Sometimes this "saying" really constitutes a command, as when God "said" to Abram to leave his home to go to a place God would later indicate (Gen. 12:1).

Indeed, since God is the sovereign Lord, none of His speech merely passes on information, however relevant, to man. Everything the sovereign God says carries divine authority. It is noteworthy that in John 1:1 ("In the beginning was the word"), *the word* (God's "saying") which was in the beginning (clearly a reference to Gen. 1:1) is distinct from God and yet *with* God, as an equal to Him. The Word through whom the creation came to be is Jesus Christ (1 Cor. 8:6).

NASB, NKJV: Then God said
NIV, RSV: And God said
LB: Then God said

51
Gog and Magog (Rev. 20:8)
GREEK: *ton Gōg kai Magōg*

This phrase occurs in the New Testament only in Rev. 20:8, although the names appear in Ezek. 38:2. The Greek phrase consists of a definite article (*ton*, specifying this as something the reader would already know about) and two proper nouns joined by the conjunction *kai* ("and"). Such a construction binds the two nouns together into a single unit. Most scholars argue that "God and Magog" in Rev. 20:8 refers to the Gog and Magog of Ezek. 38:2.

Gog, the ruler of Magog and prince of Meshech and Tubal, is mentioned in Ezek. 38:3, 14, 16, 18; 39:1, 11, 15, and the territory (or the people living in his realm) is mentioned in Ezek. 39:6. Gog is depicted as head of a sinister, if not demonic, host that he led against Israel. God defeats them decisively on Canaan's mountains (Ezek. 38-39). Several attempts have been made to identify Gog with some particular known historical person, but without decisive results. Since the Lydian King Gyges was known as *Gugu* in Assyrian texts and probably in Persian also, the name may be traceable to that dynasty of Asia Minor, which began about 685 B.C.

But perhaps the most attractive application is to the Seleucids of the days of Antiochus Epiphanes. The use of an earlier name in later literature was common, as it avoided the possible political problems of using the actual name. There are many instances of this type of usage in nearly all ancient literatures. The Hellenistic kingdom of the Seleucids centered in Northern Syria, but included ancient Meshech and Tubal in Asia Minor. If that is the case, then Magog would be Syria. According to Ezekiel, Gog's army includes troops from Meshech and Tubal, Persia, Cush, Put, Gomer, Dedan, and Tarshish. In Rev. 20:7-9 the figure of Gog and his hosts (Magog), troops from all over the earth, array themselves against the church and the holy city. As in Ezekiel, God utterly destroys them. This time they are cast into the lake of fire. Throughout the history of biblical interpretation the great anti-Christian political states have been identified with Gog and Magog.

Some believe the figures refer to Russia and the hosts that will follow her as she attacks Jerusalem. For others this is a symbolic description depicting an event yet future whose protagonist is either Israel or the church and the antagonists (respectively) either some unidentified nations or the satanic hordes. Still others see here a general figure, representing the ongoing battle between the church and its foes.

All the versions cited read "Gog and Magog."

52
Golgotha ... a place of a skull (Matt. 27:33)
GREEK: *Golgotha ... kraniou topos*

The site of Jesus' crucifixion is given in Matt. 27:33; Mark 15:22; and John 19:17. Strong interest in finding the site goes back for centuries. The text of the New Testament gives only the briefest description—the place-name Golgotha (Aramaic *Golgota*) explained with the two terms *kraniou* ("skull") and *topos* ("place"). The Latin Vulgate translated *kraniou* into Latin as *calvaria*, which was carried into English. Wycliffe's version (1380) reads "and their camen into a place, that is clepide golgatha, that is the place of caluari." From this name, "Calvary" passed into English, although it is nowhere found in Scripture. It was dropped from the versions of Tyndale (1534) and Cranmer (1539) but retained in the Rheims version of 1582.

NASB, NKJV: Golgotha ... Place of a Skull
NIV: Golgotha ... The Place of the Skull
RSV: Golgotha ... the place of a skull
LB: Golgotha ... "Skull Hill"

53
good will toward men (Luke 2:14)
GREEK: *en anthrōpois eudokias*

Only in Luke 2:14. The preposition *en*, which introduces the phrase, here bears a local meaning rather than a directional one; that is, it means "among" rather than "to" or "toward." That idea is consistent with the immediate context. The plural noun *anthrōpois* is in a locative construction and is modified by *eudokias*, a singular noun in the genitive or descriptive case. The KJV and NKJV adopt the nominative reading *eudokia*, making it the subject of the sentence parallel to *eirēnē* ("peace").

But the reasons for rejecting that reading are quite convincing. The text should read "among men of *eudokia*." *Eudokia* is to be understood as a state of well-pleased satisfaction. Clearly, it refers to God's good pleasure, not man's. The angels were not singing of peace (salvation) among men who please God (men of good will who do the right thing), for that would really be praising man. Rather, they were singing of God's good pleasure and voicing a recurrent New Testament theme (Matt. 11:26; Luke 10:21; Eph. 1:4-5, 9). Their song is a declaration of peace on earth "among men whom God has graciously chosen" (see William Hendriksen, *Exposition of the Gospel According to Luke*, 156). *God* is well pleased with *them*. The angels sang of the true and lasting peace that rests only on those whom God has chosen (Isa. 26:3, 12; 32:17; Luke 1:78-79; John 14:27; Rom. 5:1; Eph. 2:14, 17; Col. 1:20). By ascribing to God the whole work of salvation, they declare His glory, and only His glory, revealed in the birth of the Savior (Pss. 32:1; 89:33-34; John 6:44; 15:16; Eph. 1:4).

The treatment of this phrase in the various versions is instructive. The Latin Vulgate reads: *in terra pax hominibus bonae voluntatis* ("on earth peace to men of good will"), which Wycliffe (1380) follows ("in erthe pees be to men of good wille"). However, Tyndale (1534) departs from that tradition and translates "and peace on the erthe: and unto men reioysynge." Cranmer's version (1539) softens the meaning a bit more as it reads "and peace on the erth, and unto men a good wyll." In the first issue of the KJV in 1611 the word order was changed, and the well known but incorrect form of the phrase was introduced.

NASB: peace among men with whom He is pleased (note: Lit., "of His good
       pleasure"; or possibly, "of good will")
NIV: on earth peace to men on whom his favor rests
NKJV: on earth peace, good will toward men
RSV: peace among men with whom he is pleased (note: "peace, good will
       among men")
LB: and peace on earth for all those pleasing him

54
gopher wood (Gen. 6:14)
HEBREW: ʿāṣê-gōper

This phrase occurs only in Gen. 6:14. It consists of a plural construct noun followed by a singular absolute noun (literally, "woods of gopher"). The primary meaning of ʿēṣ is "tree," but it clearly refers to wood as in this passage, as it does in Ex. 15:25; Deut. 16:21, and several other places. *Gōper* is the proper name of the wood from which the ark was constructed by Noah and his family. Only the name of the wood is certain; its exact identity is unclear. Some have argued that *gōper* should be amended to *kōper* and understood as meaning "pitch." Hence, a "wood of pitch," or resin, was used. On that basis the wood is identified as one of the conifers or as cypress. But archaeological and textual evidence tends to indicate that early Sumerian and pre-Sumerian sailing craft were reed boats and that *gōper* can be interpreted in that fashion.

NASB, RSV: gopher wood
NIV: cypress wood
NKJV: gopher-wood
LB: resinous wood

E. Ullendorf, "The Construction of Noah's Ark," *Vetus Testamentum* #4, pp. 95-96.

55

Great is Diana [Artemis] of the Ephesians (Acts 19:28)
GREEK: *megalē hē Artemis Ephesiōn*

This phrase occurs only in Acts 19:28. Grammatically it consists of an adjective (*megalē*), followed by the definite article (*hē*) introducing the noun *Artemis*, which is modified by the noun *Ephesiōn*. The definite article points to a particular Artemis, known and loved by the speakers. The genitive is either of possession or identification. If the former, the speakers claim this particular goddess as uniquely theirs—the interpretation archaeology leads us to favor. The phrase may be translated either "great Artemis of the Ephesians" or "Great is Artemis of the Ephesians." The Greek goddess Artemis was accepted and worshiped by the Romans under the name *Diana*.

The name *Artemis* is not Greek, and this goddess seems to have been worshiped in Ephesus even before the Greeks arrived. There are strong similarities between her and the Semite deities Asherah, Astarte, and Ishtar. They may be the same deity, adapted to fit local situations and cultures. Artemis was the goddess of the uncultivated land, the forests and hills, and of wild things, and was the virgin huntress armed with bow and arrow. In Ephesus she was also the goddess of childbirth and probably fertility.

The enormous Ephesian temple of Artemis was one of the seven wonders of the ancient world. Young girls in saffron dresses danced before her image in imitation of bears, and temple priestesses clad in short skirts, with one breast exposed like the Amazon women, brought food and other provisions to the image. Tourists flocked to the temple and purchased countless small models of the temple made by local silversmiths. It was such craftsmen who stirred up the crowd against Paul and led the outcry "Great is Artemis of the Ephesians!"

NASB, NIV, RSV: Great is Artemis of the Ephesians
NKJV, LB: Great is Diana of the Ephesians

H

hand of the Lord (1 Chron. 21:13)
  HEBREW: *yad-yhwh*

Key passages revealing the meaning of this phrase are 1 Chron. 21:13; Josh. 4:24; and Pss. 8:6; 10:12; 95:7. It consists of a singular noun in the construct followed by a noun in the absolute. Inasmuch as God has no bodily parts, such as hands, as He clearly and repeatedly says (Deut. 4:15-19; John 4:24), the phrase "hand of the Lord" is obviously an anthropomorphism. *YHWH* (Yahweh or Jehovah) is God's covenantal name, signifying the One who gives and fulfills the covenants. Hence, it has overtones of sovereignty, self-determination, and electing love. Known by this name from the creation (Gen. 4:1), God enriched its significance in Moses' day by explaining it more fully (Ex. 6:3) and by demonstrating its implications through delivering Israel from Egypt.

The phrase bears many connotations that are strongly interrelated. (1) Often "God's hand" refers to His creativity as a craftsman (Ps. 8:6; cf. 28:4), whose creations are uniquely His possessions. An elliptical use of this connotation is seen in Ps. 109:27—"That they might know that this is [the work of] thy hand." (2) God's hand often represents His power, seen in what He has done and is able to do. Through the Exodus God showed the nations His sovereign might (Josh. 4:24). His power is never limited, so that He is always able to deliver His people (Num. 11:23; Isa. 59:1). His hand gives protection and care for those who belong to Him in a special, covenantal way (Ps. 31:5, 15). (3) God's hand suggests His authority, His divine prerogative to use His power as He sees fit. When God shakes his hand, it is a sign of warning (Isa. 10:32), and He raises it in taking an oath (Ex. 6:4). (4) God's hand represents His help, and the psalmist beseeches God to lift up His hand in behalf of those in need (Ps. 10:12; cf. 104:28; 145:16). (5) Being in God's hand can simply mean belonging to Him. In Ps. 95:7 Israel is depicted as being the sheep of His hand, a position that summons her to godliness.

NASB, NKJV, RSV: hand of the Lord
NIV, LB: hands of the Lord

57
but I will **harden his [Pharaoh's] heart** (Ex. 4:21)
    HEBREW: *wa'ᵉnî 'ăhazzēq 'et-libbô*

The full clause appears only in Ex. 4:21, though a similar one appears in other places, with YHWH being substituted for "I" (see 9:12; 10:20, 27; 11:10; 14:4, 8, 17). The clause consists of the subject, first person singular pronoun, preceded by the conjunction, the verb in the first person singular of the intensive form, and finally the sign of the direct object *'et* and the direct object itself. Before Moses approached Pharaoh, God told him what the king's response would be—that he would not let the people go until after the tenth plague. God also told him why Pharaoh would respond in this way—because God would harden his heart. In Ex. 7:3 the same idea appears, using the root *qāshāh*, causative stem, meaning "to be hard, insensitive, unresponding." God's control of Pharaoh's disposition preceded and determined the ruler's response.

In Rom. 9:14-19 Paul states this hardening work of God as a universal principle, arguing that, just as God controlled Pharaoh, so He controls all men. He specifically quotes Ex. 9, "For this very purpose I raised you up, to demonstrate my power in you, and that my name might be proclaimed throughout the whole earth" (vv. 16-17). God has mercy on whom He desires and hardens whom He desires (v. 18). The mystery of the relationship between God's sovereign election or reprobation and human responsibility is not to be examined any further, as Paul makes plain. Who can resist God's will? Obviously, no one; and God will do with the works of His hands as He pleases (Rom. 9:19-21). Yet Scripture also makes clear that men make decisions according to their own desires, wants, and inclinations. We read ten times that Pharaoh hardened his own heart (e.g., Ex. 8:15). For similar cases of God's hardening hearts, see Ex. 14:17; Deut. 2:30; Josh. 11:20.

    NASB, NIV, NKJV, RSV: harden his heart
    LB: I will make him stubborn

58
Have mercy on us, O Lord (Matt. 20:30)
    GREEK: *kurie eleēson hēmas*

This short phrase is found only in Matt. 20:30-31 as the cry of two blind men sitting on the roadside as Jesus traveled from Jericho on his way to the triumphal entry into Jerusalem. The phrase consists of the Greek title *kurie* ("Lord") in the vocative case of direct address and the verb *eleēson* ("have mercy") in the imperative aorist. The last word in the phrase is the masculine plural pronoun *hēmas* ("us") in the accusative case as the object of the verb. The special past tense indicates a simple past occurrence, with no limitations as to time of completion. The plea for mercy is thus requested for sins and hardships in effect at the time of the statement. This supplication is a direct quotation of Ps. 123:3 from the Septuagint (Greek) version. The Hebrew repeats the phrase and is translated literally, "Have mercy on us, O Jehovah; have mercy on us!"

The two blind beggars on the dirty, dusty road from Jericho addressed Jesus with this ancient prayer to Jehovah, clearly indicating that they considered Jesus, the object and focus of their belief, to be divine. The miracle that followed was the direct response of Jesus to their faith. The change from the name of God addressed in the psalm (the sacred, unspeakable, covenant name, Jehovah, or Yahweh) to the more common "Lord" had profound significance in the extension of the gospel to the Gentiles. The phrase *kurie, eleēson hēmas* became one of the most familiar prayers of the Christian church throughout the centuries. The Latin Vulgate translates the phrase as the well-known *Domine miserere nostri.* Early English versions altered the word order, so that Wycliffe (1380) and Tyndale (1534) read: "Thou Lord, the son of David, have mercy on us." The Rheims Version (1582) follows the word order of the Latin Vulgate, which in turn follows the Greek ("Lord, have mercy upon us").

NASB: Lord, have mercy on us
NIV: Lord, Son of David, have mercy on us
NKJV: Have mercy on us, 0 Lord, Son of David
RSV: Have mercy on us, Son of David
LB: Sir, King David's Son, have mercy on us

59
The heaven, even the heavens, are the Lord's (Ps. 115:16)
HEBREW: *hashshāmayim shāmayim*

Found only in Ps. 115:16, this phrase consists of the repetition of a plural noun, in the first occurrence preceded by a definite article. The following translations suggest the variety of possibilities: (1) appositional, "heaven, even the heavens," (2) predicative, "heavens are the Lord's heavens," (3) construct, "heaven of heavens," (4) superlative, "the highest heavens," and (5) the emphatic, "the heaven, even the heavens." The fifth rendering is preferred, since it best reflects the significance of the Hebrew repetition.

The word *shāmayim* (in Hebrew always in the plural) may denote either the physical heavens (Gen. 1:1) or the abode of God (Deut. 26:15). The latter meaning appears in Ps. 115:16.

The phrase denotes the outermost and highest spheres. It consists of a noun in the construct form, followed by the same noun in the absolute form, and is preceded by the definite article. Occurring seven times in Scripture, it always refers to the abode of God, in contrast to the sphere of the created universe represented by "earth" (Deut. 10:14). This dwelling place is uniquely God's creation (Neh. 9:6) and possession (Deut. 10:14), and is summoned (that is, its inhabitants are summoned) to praise God (Ps. 148:4). God is not contained in or by this abode, or by anything He has created (1 Kings 8:27). He is limitless and omnipresent. Ps. 68:34 applies to God an epithet ("rider of the clouds") often used of Baal in Ugaritic literature, except that in the psalm God is the rider, the supreme controller, of the highest and most ancient heavens. The psalmist exalts God over the pagan deity and completely denies Baal's very existence.

NASB: The heavens are the heavens of the Lord
NIV: The highest heavens belong to the Lord
NKJV: The heaven, even the heavens, are the Lord's
RSV: The heavens are the Lord's heavens
LB: The heavens belong to the Lord

60
he himself is Christ a King (Luke 23:2)
GREEK: *heauton christon basileia einai*

This statement appears in Luke 23:2 and was attributed to Jesus by members of the Jewish Sanhedrin when they brought Him before Pilate for judgment. The same event is described in Matt. 27:2 and John 18:28-37, but the statement is not included. The original language of the phrase was no doubt Aramaic, but was likely given to Pilate in Greek, the lingua franca of the Eastern Mediterranean. The three key words are *christon basileia einai*—literally, "Christ a king to be," or more idiomatically, "to be Christ, a king"—and reflect both the sacrificial and authoritative aspect of the incarnation. *Christos* is the Greek equivalent of the Hebrew *Messiah*, meaning "the anointed one," and *basileia* means "king" in all periods of the Greek language. This phrase proves beyond any question that Jesus was understood by His contemporaries to claim messiahship and divine kingship for Himself.

NASB, NKJV: He Himself is Christ, a King
NIV: to be Christ, a king
RSV: Christ a king
LB: is our Messiah—a King

61
high places (Lev. 26:30)
HEBREW: 'et-bāmōtêkem

In its first biblical appearance (Lev. 26:30), this phrase is introduced with the sign of the direct object (*et*). The noun tself, *bāmōtêkem*, is a plural with a suffix, and basically means a "high place" or "ridge," such as the top or side of a hill (see, e.g., Deut. 33:29; Isa. 15:2). Its most frequent meaning, however (used some 80 times in the Old Testament), denotes places of cultic worship, which were usually on elevated ground. Inasmuch as a *bāmôt* could also be in a valley (Jer. 7:31), the word represents activity or use more than location. It was usually a place of pagan worship, although it was sometimes used of a proper Israelite place of worship, especially prior to the building of the Temple in Jerusalem (see 1 Sam. 9:12; 1 Kings 3:2).

Most often located atop hills and other heights, pagan cultic places included idols (2 Chron. 33:19) and *ashērāh* (wooden poles or stele symbolizing the goddess of fertility), a *maṣṣēbāh* (a stone pillar representing the male god or the dead; see 2 Kings 3:2), an altar of stones (see 2 Kings 21:3), and a room or tent used to house cultic vessels and to host sacrificial meals (see 1 Kings 12:31). Large altars made of layers of stones have been excavated at Megiddo and Hazor. Six worship activities are attested: burning incense, general sacrificing, eating cultic meals, praying, prostitution as union with the goddess of life and prosperity, and child sacrifice by passing through fire (see Lev. 18:21; 2 Kings 17:17; Jer. 19:5). Israelite worship at the *bāmôt* strengthened unbelief in the true God, gave reverence to all that He forbade in His law, symbolized union with evil (1 Cor. 10:19-21), and was denounced and judged by Him (Lev. 26:30; Ezek. 6:3). Pagan worship not only rejected God but, with its cult prostitution and child sacrifice, was a frontal attack on the family and on society as a whole.

NASB, NIV, NKJV, RSV: high places
LB: altars on the hills

I

62
if he will perform unto thee the part of a kinsman (Ruth 3:13)
HEBREW: *im yigʿālēk*

The particular form of the Hebrew verb bearing this meaning appears only in Ruth 3:13, and is an imperfect third masculine singular, with an affixed second person singular suffix. The root *gāʾal* is used in relation to five basic situations: (1) the responsibility of a kinsman to redeem (buy back) a man, or a man's family or property, which has passed to another due to extreme poverty (Lev. 25:25); (2) a kinsman's responsibility to redeem a person or thing dedicated to the Lord (Lev. 27:11); (3) the responsibility to take the life of anyone who murders a kinsman (Num. 35:12); (4) the act of God by which He vindicates and redeems (reestablishes in covenant) His people (Isa. 43:1-3); and (5) the responsibility of the nearest male kinsman to father a son by the wife of a deceased and childless relative (called a levirate marriage). It is this last sense that applies in Ruth 3:13.

The first mention of levirate marriage is in Gen. 38:8, and the Mosaic law recognized the practice. A son from such a marriage was both the heir of the deceased and son of the kinsman, the *levir* (a Latin term for "husband's brother"). If the kinsman refused to marry the widow, she was to remove his shoe in public, spit in his face, and declare him shameful for not "building his brother's house." Thereafter, this shame would follow him (Deut. 25:5-10). Levirate marriage was still practiced in Jesus' day (see Matt. 22:23-33).

NASB: if he will redeem you
NIV: if he wants to redeem
NKJV: perform the duty of a near kinsman for you
RSV: if he will do the part of the next of kin for you
LB: if he will marry you

63
I have surely seen (Ex. 3:7)
HEBREW: *rāʾōh raʾîtî*

This phrase is typical of a Hebrew usage quite foreign to Indo-European languages such as Greek, Latin, German, and English. It uses two forms of the same verb, the first an infinitive absolute and the second a finite. Such phrases were used to strengthen the meaning of the verb. In Ex. 3:7 the literal meaning is "Seeing, I have seen."

Following are some of the better known of such phrases used in the Old Testament (given first with their literal, and then with their more idiomatic, English renderings): "dying, you shall die," "you shall certainly die" (Gen. 2:17); "returning, I shall return," "I shall certainly return" (Gen. 18:10); "becoming, shall become great," "shall certainly become great" (Gen. 18:18); and a double usage in Gen 22:17—"that in blessing I will bless you and in multiplying I will multiply your heirs," "that I will certainly bless you and I will certainly multiply your heirs." Similar uses are found in Gen. 28:22; 43:3; Amos 5:5; 9:8.

Double use of such phrases often occurs in God's promises, as in that to Abraham (Gen. 22:17). In these contexts the construction gives the highest authority and weight to the words of God and of His messengers. In 1 Sam. 9:6 the emphasis is particularly strong, speaking of Samuel—"Look now, there is in this city a man of God, and he is a man who is held in respect, for all he says coming to pass, comes to pass." As would be expected, the full force of the Hebrew is not always brought out in translation.

NASB: I have surely seen the affliction
NIV: I have indeed seen the misery
NKJV: I have surely seen the oppression
RSV: I have seen the affliction
LB: I have seen the deep sorrows

64

To an **inheritance incorruptible, and undefiled, and that fadeth not away** (1 Pet. 1:4)

GREEK *eis klēronomian aphtharton kai amianton kai amaranton*

Appearing only in 1 Pet. 1:4, this phrase consists of the preposition *eis* followed by its object, the noun *klēronomian* (accusative singular), which is modified by three adjectives (all accusative singular). The idea of an inheritance as the end or goal of salvation is seen even in the early accounts of the Old Testament. Abraham searched for the city "whose builder and maker is God" (Heb. 11:10; cf. Gen. 12:3; Gal. 3:6). The faithful of Israel one day would see the land of Palestine as their inheritance (Ex. 32:13), but their supreme heritage was God Himself (Josh. 18:7; Ezek. 47:22; Heb. 4). This inheritance consists of the kingdom of

God in all its fulfilled perfection (Heb. 9:15). Peter refers to it as salvation (1 Pet. 1:9), grace, or grace of life (1:13; 3:7), glory (5:1), unfading crown of glory (5:4), and eternal glory of God (5:10). The inheritance of believers is incorruptible (not subject to decay) and thus imperishable and immortal (not subject to destruction or death). It is undefiled (not stained with defect) and unfading (not diminishing in beauty). Therefore the hope of all saints of all ages (Heb. 11:39-40) is an eternal, heavenly inheritance that is incorruptible in substance, undefiled in purity, and unfading in beauty.

NASB: an inheritance which is imperishable and undefiled and will not fade away

NIV: an inheritance that can never perish, spoil or fade

NKJV: an inheritance incorruptible and undefiled and that does not fade away

RSV: an inheritance which is imperishable, undefiled, and unfading

LB: the priceless gift of eternal life; it is kept in heaven for you, pure and undefiled, and beyond the reach of change and decay

65
So God created man **in his own image** (Gen. 1:27)
HEBREW: *wayyibrā' 'ĕlōhîm 'et-hā'ādām bᵉṣalmô*

This phrase occurs only in Gen. 1:27, although its equivalent is found in Gen. 1:26 and 9:6. The clause containing the phrase consists of the Hebrew prefix for "and" (or "so") joined to an imperfect third person singular of the verb *bārā'* followed by the direct object (*'ādām*). This noun is preceded by the sign of the direct object (*'et*) and the definite article *hā* and is closed by the prepositional phrase *bᵉṣalmô*. *Bārā'* ("create" or "make") is used in the base stem only of God's activities. In Ps. 104:30 it speaks of the ongoing process of the renewal of life, the bringing forth of creatures. In the Genesis creation account and subsequent references this word has overtones of what is known as *creatio ex nihilo*, creation from nothing (cf. Gen. 1:1 below; also 21, 27; 3:1; etc.). The decisive evidence for *creatio ex nihilo* stems particularly from Gen. 1:1, from such passages as Rom. 11:36 ("for of him and through him and to him are all things"; cf. 1 Cor. 8:6; 11:12; Col. 1:16; Heb. 2:10), and from the Bible's insistence throughout that its God is the only God, the only true deity (e.g., Isa. 44:24).

We do not see *creatio ex nihilo* directly in the creation of man, since God formed him from the dust of the ground. But that from which man was made was created from nothing and was formed into God's own image and likeness. In his spiritual, moral, and intellectual likeness to

God (Ps. 8:5-8) man was given dominion over the rest of creation. Since God is nonmaterial and has no body (Deut. 4:15-19), this image of God does not involve man's body. Man was created in God's image, but he never partook of the divine nature as such. He was and remains a creature in all his attributes. The Fall greatly defaced the image of God in man, depriving him of moral perfection, much intellectual comprehension, and spiritual kinship with God. Yet there remained in man a general sense, an intellectual and presuppositional awareness of God's existence, and a spiritual hunger for his Creator (Rom. 1:18-23; 2:14-15).

NASB, NIV, RSV: in His (his) own image
NKJV: in His own image
LB: like his Maker

66
In the beginning God created (Gen. 1:1)
HEBREW: *bᵉrēʾshît bārāʾ ʾelōhîm*

This phrase occurs only in Gen. 1:1 and consists of a prepositional phrase (used adverbially) followed by the verb (singular perfect, representing completed action). Followed by "heavens and earth" (a phrase representing all that is created), the passage argues conclusively for *creatio ex nihilo* (creation out of nothing). Much debate has surrounded these words, and many scholars (including some modern translators) have rendered the prepositional phrase with "when" (e.g., "In the beginning when God created the universe," *Good News Bible*). The rendering is based primarily on the identification of this phrase with *enuma elish*, the words with which the Babylonian epic of creation opens. But such an identification is unjustified (see W. White, "Enuma Elish," *The Zondervan Pictorial Bible Encyclopedia*, 2:314). Other biblical occurrences and the testimony of all ancient versions reinforce the traditional translation of simply "in the beginning," which marks the initiation of a series of historical events. Especially relevant for Christians is John 1:1, which includes a translation of the Hebrew phrase.

Although the verb *bārāʾ* may be used of renewal rather than *creatio ex nihilo* (as in Ps. 51:10) and of creating by combining preexisting matter with that which did not previously exist (as in Gen. 1:26-27; Ps. 104:1-10), it often connotes original creative action (as in Ex. 34:10; Isa. 41:20; 48:6-7; 65:17). The force of the Gen. 1:1 clause is to set forth a particular event when all that is created ("heavens and earth") came into existence. This significance is buttressed by passages such as Rom. 1:20; 11:36; and Heb. 2:10 and by the Bible's insistence that God is the only Creator (Isa. 44:24).

NASB, NIV, NKJV, RSV: In the beginning God created
LB: When God began creating

67

In the end of the sabbath (Matt. 28:1)

GREEK: *opse de sabbatōn*

This phrase occurs only in Matt. 28:1 and consists of the preposition *opse*, which can mean either "late on" or "after," both of which meanings are attested in Greek literature. A comparison of the other gospels leads to the conclusion that here *opse* means "after" (see Mark 16:1; Luke 24:1; John 20:1). The post-positive article *de* is properly rendered "now" in several translations. The plural noun *sabbatōn* may mean either a particular day, "the Sabbath day," or "week." In either case, the meaning is the same, signifying early Sunday morning at first light.

NASB, NKJV: Now after the Sabbath
NIV: After the Sabbath
RSV: Now after the sabbath
LB: Early on Sunday morning

68

in the last days (Acts 2:17)

GREEK: *en tais eschatais hēmerais*

This phrase first occurs in Acts 2:17, as a citation of Joel 2:28. It refers to the present Christian era as the final period, or as part of the final period, of history. The peoples of antiquity thought of themselves as living at the end of a long historical experience and envisioned the times after them as being late in history. The Greek phrase opens with a preposition *en*, denoting temporal location. The noun *hemerais* is in the locative case and is modified by the definite article *tais*, indicating reference to the "last days" already known (i.e., from the Old Testament). The adjective *eschatais* simply means "last," as in our word *eschatology*, the study of the last things.

This phrase also occurs in the singular, appearing first in John 6:39 ("at the last day"). The basic idea is expressed in "last time" (1 John 2:18) and "last time" (1 Pet. 1:5). The singular form (used seven times) often refers to the day of judgment, at the very end of time. The plural and its conceptual equivalents (except in 1 John 2:18 and Jude 18) refer to the New Testament era as the consummation of the Old Testament era (see Isa. 2:2; Hos. 3:5; etc.). It is the time prophesied (Acts 2:17), the period in which the perfect revelation of God has appeared (Heb. 1:2) and in which we now live (2 Tim. 3:1; James 5:3; 1 Pet. 1:20; 2 Pet. 3:3).

All versions cited read "In the last days."

Nigel Turner, *Christian Words* (Nashville: Nelson, 1982), pp. 137-41.

69
it shall bruise thy head (Gen. 3:15)
HEBREW: *y^eshûpkā r'ōsh*

This phrase is found only in Gen. 3:1, although the verb *shûp* also appears in Gen. 3:15; Job 9:17; and Ps. 139:11. Our phrase consists of the verb with an appended personal pronoun followed by the noun *rōsh* (literally, "he shall bruise you with reference to the head"). Gen. 3:15 is often called the *protevangelium*, the first good news of a Savior, who would destroy the devil and all his works. The phrase *shûp* means "bruise," and refers to a fatal blow, that is, a blow on the head brought upon the serpent (the devil). In context this connotes the total destruction of the serpent and his followers and all they have accomplished. God's glory will be vindicated and totally displayed through the Savior to come. By contrast the serpent (Satan) will only bruise the Redeemer on the heel, a minor blow. Some scholars would read this second *shûp* as "snatch" or "snap," even "to gasp" or "pant after." But there is no need to change the root or translation. That Christ fatally wounded the serpent is clear from the New Testament, even as it is clear that the serpent registered a wound on Christ's heel in the crucifixion. The finality of Satan's wound is yet to be realized (Rom. 16:20; Rev. 20).

NASB: He shall bruise you on the head
NIV: he will crush your head
NKJV: He shall bruise your head
RSV: he shall bruise your head
LB: He shall strike you on your head

J

Jesus perceived their thoughts (Luke 5:22)
GREEK: *epignous de ho Iēsous tous dialogismous autōn*

This phrase has near equivalents in Luke 6:8 and 1 Cor. 3:20 (a citation of Ps. 94:11), except that in the first passage the Greek verb is a form of *oida* and in the second a form of *ginōskō*. The compound *epiginōskō* is also best taken in the simple sense of "know" or, connotatively, "perceive." The aorist, a type of past participle, places the time of Jesus' perception as antecedent to His questioning the scribes and Pharisees. The definite article *ho* makes it certain that Jesus is the subject. The noun *dialogismous* refers to the thoughts in the all-inclusive sense of "opinions," "reasonings," or "designs." As God, Jesus knew what was in the minds of men (Matt. 9:4; 12:25; Mark 2:8; John 1:47-48; 2:25). He knew their inmost thoughts, so nothing was hidden from Him (see Ps. 139; Heb. 4:13).

NASB: Jesus, aware of their reasonings
NIV, LB: Jesus knew what they were thinking
NKJV: But when Jesus perceived their thoughts
RSV: When Jesus perceived their questionings

Jesus of Nazareth (Matt. 26:71)
GREEK: *Iēsou tou Nazōraiou*

The phrase consists of a noun (here in the genitive case, because in the Greek text it is the object of a preposition) modified by the noun *Nazōraiou*, which is made definite by the article *tou*. This phrase and its near equivalents occur 19 times in the New Testament, all indicating the place of Jesus' residence—that He was from Nazareth. (It does not identify Him as one under the Nazirite vow, as was Samson.) Compare, for example, "Saul of Tarsus." First century Nazarenes were despised by their fellow Jews in Galilee (John 1:46; see phrase "Galilee of the Gentiles"), and Jesus' being looked down on as a Nazarene (Matt. 2:23) fulfilled Isa. 53. Most Nazarenes were of mixed blood, spoke a rough dialect, and were known to the Herodians for sedition and rebellion. In the court outside the Sanhedrin's meeting place the designation seems to have been used with scorn, bearing all the negative associations of the religiously and politically turbulent and troublesome village (see Matt. 26:71; Mark 14:67).

Knowing the town's reputation, it was no doubt with deliberate irony that Pilate inscribed over the cross "JESUS OF NAZARETH THE KING OF THE JEWS" (John 19:19). A seemingly insignificant person, rejected by His own people, was now publicly and scornfully declared to be king of the Jews. For many who saw and knew of Jesus' miracles, however, His being a Nazarene carried no stigma. The sick called out to Jesus the Nazarene (Mark 10:47; Luke 18:37). And in view of His mighty vindication through the resurrection (Acts 2:2; 10:38), this designation of Jesus was used proudly by early Christians.

NASB, RSV: This man was with Jesus of Nazareth
NIV: This fellow was with Jesus of Nazareth
NKJV: This fellow also was with Jesus of Nazareth
LB: This man was with Jesus—from Nazareth

K

King of kings, and Lord of lords (1 Tim. 6:15)
GREEK: *ho basileus tōn basileuontōn kai kurios tōn kurieuontōn*

This significant phrase is used in 1 Tim. 6:15 and Rev. 17:14, in the scene of the victory of the militant and triumphant Christ. Although it appears in the Greek of the New Testament, it was a standard Semitic expression. The construction supplies the superlative degree of nouns and adjectives, for which Semitic languages have no simple inflected form. The standard arrangement is: noun + "of" + plural of the noun, a classic example of which is in 1 Tim. 6:15 ("King of kings"). The comparison in English is simple enough to understand.

Noun:	great king	greater king	king of kings
Degree:	absolute	compara-tive	superlative

Interestingly enough, classical Greek had a form for the superlative degree. The absolute of "king" was *basileus* and the superlative was *basiletatos* ("greatest king"). But in 1 Tim. 6:15 and Rev. 17:14 the Greek uses the Hebrew form, and literally means "a king of the kings"—that is, the greatest of kings. Although there are many other examples in Scripture, the full superlative meaning is usually lost in translation. One of the most commonly misunderstood of these superlative phrases is the title of the book commonly called *The Song of Solomon*. The Hebrew title follows the standard for of noun + "of" + plural noun (*shîr ha-shîrîm*)—literally "Song of the Songs," or "The Greatest Song." Other examples are found in Gen. 9:25 ("servant of servants," or "most servile servant"); 1 Kings 8:27 ("heaven of heavens," or "highest heaven"); and the difficult passage in Isa 34:10 ("forever of forevers"; actually, "farthest forever," or better, "most distant forever").

The Greek form becomes a common doxology in the New Testament (see Gal. 1:5; Phil. 4:20; 1 Tim. 1:17; 2 Tim. 4:18; Heb 1:8; 13:21; 1 Pet. 4:11; 5:11). It is used twelve times in Revelation. In the Old Testament several of the most significant phrases in the Israelite worship service are of this type—"highest of holies" (Ex. 26:33) and "most sacred Sabbath" (Ex. 31:15).

The versions cited follow the KJV in most cases.

73

the kingdom is the Lord's: and he is the governor among the nations (Ps. 22:28 [H v. 29])

HEBREW: *kî layhwh hammᵉlûkāh / ûmōshēl baggôyim*

The phrase occurs only in Ps. 22:28 (H v. 29). The first clause consists of the particle *kî* (which here opens the clause as a strong asseverative); the prepositional phrase, used adverbially and composed of the preposition *l* (indicating possession or identity), with its object (the proper name *YHWH*); and the subject, the abstract noun *mᵉlûkāh* ("kingdom"), prefixed by the definite article *ha*. The second clause poetically parallels the first, and consists of a participle used denominatively and modified and a prepositional phrase (the preposition *ba* and the plural noun *gôyim*, meaning "Gentile nations"). The emphasis of both clauses is on God's kingdom as His rule and dominion. This concept occurs frequently in the Old Testament and is to be distinguished from His kingdom as the realm (or political entity) over which He reigns. God has ruled over all nations as king from the beginning (Ps. 93:2 [H v. 3]).

The concept of God's kingship (rule) became more prominent with the establishment of Israel as a theocracy. As king God was the lawgiver (Deut. 33:5), law enforcer (Deut. 17:19-20; 24:15; 25:9; Jer. 10:10), and protector (Deut. 17:16; 1, Sam. 12:12). The Messiah, the Son, was to be enthroned by God as the perfect king (Ps. 2:6) and was to sit on David's throne ruling the world in justice and righteousness (Isa. 9:7; 11:1-5; etc.). His kingdom would never be destroyed, but would destroy all its enemies (Dan. 2:44). In the New Testament, Jesus declares the presence of the kingdom of God (Mark 1:15). His preaching describes it as the rule of God over the hearts of men (John 3:3; cf. Ps. 22:28) as well as a *realm* over which God rules (Matt. 16:19; 18:15-18; cf. Dan. 2:44). The end of history will see Jesus handing over the kingdom to the Father, with all His enemies conquered and all His subjects perfected (1 Cor. 15:24).

NASB: For the kingdom is the Lord's / And He rules over the nations
NIV: for dominion belongs to the Lord / and he rules over the nations
NKJV: For the kingdom is the Lord's, / And He rules over the nations
RSV: For dominion belongs to the Lord / and he rules over the nations
LB: For the Lord is King / and rules the nations

74

the kingdom of heaven (Matt. 4:17)

  GREEK: *hē basileia tōn ouranōn*

The Greek phrase consists of a definite article *hē*, its noun (nominative, feminine, singular), and the definite article *tōn* (genitive of identity) with its noun (genitive of identity plural, which modifies the first noun). The two definite articles emphasize that this kingdom and this heaven are already known to the audience (from the Old Testament). The use of the Greek plural in referring to heaven is a Semiticism (the Hebrew word for heaven is always plural). Here heaven refers to the abode of God, where He dwells and where His will is perfectly kept. It is a heavenly kingdom in origin and, therefore, in nature.

Matt. 4:23 is a crucial passage, because it tells us that the gospel of the kingdom was the substance of Christ's preaching. The message with which He began (4:17) dominated His entire ministry. It is important to note that He had a single major theme: the gospel of the kingdom, the gospel concerning the one true and perfect kingdom. According to Mark 1:15; 4:11 and Luke 4:43-44, He declared the gospel of the kingdom of *God*. Some scholars have tried to distinguish between the kingdom of heaven and the kingdom of God, but there is severe difficulty with this. A comparison of Jesus' teaching regarding the kingdom of heaven and the kingdom of God shows that at the same places and same times He said the same things about both. They are simply two phrases for one concept (compare Matt. 11:12 and Luke 16:16; Matt. 5:3 and Luke 6:20; Matt. 10:7 and Luke 9:2; Matt. 13:31 and Mark 4:30-31; Matt. 19:14 and Mark 10:14; Matt. 19:23 and Luke 18:24).

The kingdom of God has two aspects: (1) His reign or rule over men's hearts and lives (Matt. 6:10; Luke 17:21), resulting in complete salvation (Mark 10:25-26) and (2) the realm over which He reigns—the community of those who have received Christ as their King (Matt. 16:18-19), along with the entire redeemed universe (Matt. 25:34).

  NASB, NIV, NKJV, RSV: the kingdom of heaven
  LB: the Kingdom of heaven

75

knew her not till (Matt. 1:25)

  GREEK: *ouk eginōsken autēn heōs*

This phrase occurs only in Matt. 1:25. The imperfect tense indicates that, throughout the period specified in the text, Joseph did not "know"

Mary, his wife. "To know" is used of sexual relations both in the Old and New Testaments. In the Old Testament it was used of normal marital relations, referring either to man or woman (Gen. 4:1; 19:8; Num. 31:17), of rape (Judg. 19:25), or of homosexual relations (Gen. 19:5). In the New Testament the word bears sexual meaning only in Matt. 1:25 and Luke 1:34.

The doctrine of Mary's perpetual virginity is challenged by these passages—that is, by the combination of "was not knowing" and "until." Grammatically this suggests (although it does not demand) that, after the birth of Jesus, Mary and Joseph had normal marital relations. That such was actually the case is established by the facts that (1) God instituted marriage in part that children might result (Gen. 1:28), (2) God commands married couples to bring forth children (Gen. 1:28), (3) God often blesses obedient married couples with many children (Ps. 127:3), (4) God forbids prolonged sexual abstinence between marriage partners (1 Cor. 7:5), (5) God pronounces marriage honorable and the marriage bed (sexual relations) undefiled (Heb. 13:4), (6) Jesus had brothers and sisters who clearly belonged to His immediate family and were sons and daughters of His mother (Matt. 12:46-47; Mark 3:31-32; Luke 8:19; John 2:12; 7:3, 5, 10), and (7) Jesus was Mary's firstborn son, implying that other children were also born to her (Luke 2:7).

NASB: and kept her a virgin until
NIV: he had no union with her until
NKJV: and did not know her till
RSV: knew her not until
LB: but she remained a virgin until

76

Ye shall **know them by their fruits** (Matt. 7:16)
   GREEK: *apo tōn karpōn autōn epignōsesthe autous*

This phrase occurs in Matt. 7:16, 20. The verb *ginōskō* appears with the appended preposition *epi*, which serves to heighten the meaning of the verb. False prophets ("them") will not simply be known, but will be understood and seen for what they really are—God's enemies and saboteurs of His kingdom and His people. Their fruits, which are emphatically and uniquely theirs, reveal their hidden evil intents. Such fruits certainly consist of what the prophet teaches (Isa. 8:20; Matt. 15:7; Titus 1:9-12; Heb. 13:9; 1 John 4:1-3; 2 John 9-11), and the godly are to look beyond marvelous deeds to the teaching of the prophet (Deut. 13:1-5; cf. Matt. 7:22). But "fruits" also refer to the life and behavior of these teachers (Luke 3:8-14; John 18:8-10; Gal. 5:22-24; Eph. 5:9-12; Phil. 1:11;

Col. 1:10; James 3:17-18). Jesus taught that a teacher's true character cannot long be hidden, but soon reveals itself in what he says and does (Luke 6:44-45).

NASB, NKJV, RSV: You will know them by their fruits
NIV: By their fruit you will recognize them
LB: You can detect them by the way they act

L

land of Shinar (Gen. 10:10)
HEBREW: *beʾereṣ shinʿār*

Used as a place name, this phrase appears seven times in the Old Testament (Gen. 10:10; 11:2; 14:1; 14:9; Isa. 11:11; Dan. 1:2; Zech. 5:11). In each of these contexts Mesopotamia is mentioned, and it is in this region, of what is now the seacoast of Iraq, that scholars have looked for Shinar. And, in fact, it seems to be a Semitic name for the ancient pre-Semitic empire known as Sumer. The Hebrew *shinʿār* should therefore probably always be translated "Sumer." The Sumerian empire reflected the very early culture of the Tigris and Euphrates valley and was the first known literate civilization. Since the Sumerian word for "city" was Ur(i), it has long been assumed that Ur of the Chaldeans, the ancestral home of Abraham, was the famous Sumerian city of Ur. There is evidence in the tablets from Ebla, however, that there were other towns named Ur (see phrase "Ur of the Chaldees").

NASB, NKJV, RSV: the land of Shinar
NIV: in Shinar
LB: in the land of Babylon

78
The law and the prophets (Luke 16:16)
GREEK: *ho nomos kai hoi prophētai*

A key passage for understanding this phrase is Luke 16:16. Grammatically it opens with the definite article *ho* modifying the noun *nomos*, which is followed by the conjunction and another definite article modifying the noun *prophētai*. The definite articles indicate that both the law and prophets were already known to the audience. Jews of Jesus' day knew well the phrase "the law and the prophets" as a reference to the entire Old Testament. This is affirmed by Jesus' insistence that He did not come to destroy the law and the prophets but to uphold them (Matt. 7:12). Again, Jesus taught that all the law and the prophets hung on the two primal commands to love God and one's neighbor (Matt. 7:12; 22:40). Thus, "the law" encompasses the books of Moses, often called simply "Moses" (e.g., Luke 16:29), while "the prophets" embraces the rest of the Old Testament. In Luke 24:44 the Old Testament is referred to under a threefold division: the law, the prophets, and the psalms.

NASB, NIV: The Law and the Prophets
NKJV, RSV: The law and the prophets
LB: the laws of Moses and the messages of the prophets

79
the law of Moses (John 7:23)
   GREEK: *ho nomos Mōuseōs*

This phrase consists of the definite article *ho* (by which attention is drawn to a particular and already known "law") and the noun *nomos*, modified by the proper name *Mōuseōs* (a genitive of description, masculine, singular). The phrase is common throughout biblical literature and appears at every level of the Old Testament record after Moses (e.g., Josh. 8:31; 1 Kings 2:3; 2 Kings 14:6; 23:25; Ezra 3:2; Neh. 8:1; Dan. 9:11; Mal. 4:4), and throughout the New Testament (e.g., Luke 2:22; Acts 15:5; 1 Cor. 9:9; Heb. 10:28). It refers specifically to the Pentateuch, the five books given through Moses (2 Chron. 35:12; Neh. 13:1; John 7:19) as *the* law book, the book containing God's commandments for His people. Not even one law should be broken, since such a violation breaks the whole law (Matt. 5:17-20; James 2:10). At the same time, Jesus pointed out that inherent in the law (God's system of commands) is a ranking by which one law, such as that regarding circumcision, may take precedence over another, such as that regarding the Sabbath (John 7:23). The Sabbath was to be kept (cf. Isa. 58:13; Heb. 4), but acts of mercy and necessity, as well as circumcision, were proper Sabbath activities.

NASB: the Law of Moses
NIV, NKJV, RSV: the law of Moses
LB: the Mosaic law

80
let them be for signs, and for seasons, and for days, and years (Gen. 1:14)
   HEBREW: *wᵉhāyû lᵉʾōtōt ûlmôʿādîm ûlyāmîm wᵉ šānîm*

This sequence of words, occurring only in Gen. 1:14, describes the function of the heavenly luminaries as it was divinely established from the beginning. The verb *hāyû* has the force of a command, and is a form of the Hebrew verb for "to be." The four plural words following the verb form adverbial phrases introduced by a preposition of purpose. Heavenly luminaries were created (1) to regulate the difference between nighttime and daytime, (2) to regulate the matters set forth in the phrase, and (3) to provide light, and therefore life, for earthly creatures. With regard to the phrase these lights serve as signs in a twofold sense: (1) to forecast extraordinary events (see Jer. 10:2; Matt 2:2; Luke 21:25) and divine judgments (see Jer. 10:2; Joel 2:30), and (2) to indicate changes in the weather and parts of the sky (of use, e.g., to mariners). As indicators of the seasons, or fixed definite times, the heavenly bodies indicate and regulate such things as festal seasons, agricultural periods, vegetable life, breeding seasons of animals, and the migrations of birds (see, e.g., Ps. 104:19; Jer. 8:7). They also regulate the division of days and years, providing a structure by which time may be orderly measured.

NASB: for signs, and for seasons, and for days and years
NIV: as signs to mark seasons and days and years
NKJV: for signs and seasons, and for days and years
RSV: for signs and for seasons and for days and years
LB: they shall bring about the seasons on the earth, and mark the days and years

81
leviathan the piercing serpent (Isa. 27:1)
HEBREW: *liwyātān nāḥāsh bāriaḥ*

This highly poetic phrase appears in Isa. 27:1. The full poetic lines are:

> Leviathan the evil serpent
> Leviathan the crooked serpent.

For centuries no background was known for this verse. The terms were strange and could be found nowhere in contemporary literature, until discovered in the cuneiform tablets from Ugarit. In a mythological text from before 1600 B.C. comes a set of poetic lines very similar to the passage in Isaiah.

> When you struck Lotan the evil serpent,

made an end of the crooked serpent,
Shalylt of the seven heads.

The notion of an awesome monster of the sea that is slain by the god is widely reflected in ancient Semitic literature, and apparently was part of Hebrew culture and language. The Old Testament has a number of passages representing this sort of linguistic material derived from then Near East mythologies. In no case do these uses indicate pagan religious influence, but they do indicate the antiquity and cultural level of the text.

RSV: Leviathan the twisting serpent
NASB: Even Leviathan the twisted serpent (note: Or, "sea monster")
LB: the coiling, writhing serpent
NIV: Leviathan the coiling serpent
NKJV: Leviathan the fleeing serpent

82
lifted up his eyes (Gen. 13:10)
HEBREW: *wayyiśā' . . . 'et-'ēnāw*

This phrase first occurs in Gen. 13:10, other key passages being Gen. 39:7; Num. 24:2; Deut. 4:19; 2 Kings 19:22; and Pss. 121:1; 123:1-2. It basically connotes looking intently at something and often has overtones of a panoramic view—such as Balaam's view of Israel (Num. 24:2). In passages such as 2 Kings 19:22, lifting up one's eyes means to look haughtily and proudly toward someone. Used positively, it connotes looking with desire on someone or something. Potiphar's wife lifted up her eyes to (upon) Joseph (Gen. 39:7). Lot lifted up his eyes (in desire) upon the valley of Sodom and Gomorrah (Gen. 13:10), and God encouraged Abram to look upon all Canaan as a desirable inheritance (Gen. 13:14). The phrase sometimes refers to looking upon someone or something in hope or trust (Ps. 121:1). The psalmist confessed that he lifted up his eyes to God (in hope and commitment), even as a faithful servant looks to his master (Ps. 123:1-2). Finally, the phrase may refer to an act of worship (Deut. 4:19; Ezek. 18:6).

NASB, RSV: lifted up his eyes
NIV: looked up
NKJV: lifted his eyes
LB: took a long look

83
living creature after his kind (Gen. 1:24)
HEBREW: *nepesh ḥayyāh lᵉmināh*

This phrase occurs only in Gen. 1:24, and consists of the noun *nepesh*, modified by another noun *ḥayyāh* (lit., "a *nepesh* of a *ḥayyāh*"), followed by a prepositional phrase with *mîn* ("kind") as its object. The unusual collective noun *mîn* is always used with a preposition. It has no known etymology and simply refers to a "likeness" or "sort." The word appears infrequently in the Bible (see Gen. 6:20; 7:14; Lev. 11:14; Deut. 14:13; Ezek. 47:10). *Nepesh* represents a creature that breathes, and *ḥayyāh* means "a living thing," both nouns being collective singulars. In this context the phrase refers to all animated beings other than man. Generally, the animals are classified as (1) *bᵉ hēmāh*, large land animals, (2) *remeś*, smaller land animals, and (3) *haytô ereṣ*, wild beasts of the earth, the rest of the animals. In Gen. 6:20 the third class is replaced by the birds ("flying creatures"), while in 7:14 there are four categories. It is clear that God intends the reader to see all earthly created beings except man in this list. Thus *nepesh ḥayyāh* includes all the animals and describes them as animated beings.

Then God breathed in man the breath of life, and man also became a *nepesh ḥayyāh*, a living creature, an animated being (Gen. 2:7). Each living creature was brought forth after its kind (Gen. 1:24). In Leviticus and Deuteronomy kites, falcons, ravens, ostriches, locusts, crickets, grasshoppers, etc., represent separate and distinct kinds. Therefore one should be very cautious about superimposing modern zoological classifications on the Genesis or other scriptural categories of animals. The account relates to the origin of the animals within a theological cosmology and not to their genetic relationships. Each "kind" of animal had an origin of its own.

NASB: living creatures after their kind
NIV, RSV: living creatures according to their kinds
NKJV: living creature according to its kind
LB: every kind of animal

84
LORD of hosts (Isa. 1:9)
HEBREW: *yhwh ṣᵉbā'ôt*

A primary occurrence of this phrase is in Isa. 1:9, and it consists of the divine name *YHWH* in construct relationship, followed by the plural noun ṣᵉbā᾽ôt. Sᵉbā᾽ôt ("hosts," i.e., a large group of persons) occurs 285 times after a divine name, which in 261 cases is *YHWH*. The common pronunciation "Jehovah" is derived from adding the vowels from the usual Hebrew word for "lord" (᾽ădōnay) to the consonants of the covenant name (YHWH). After the canonical period the name came to be held in such reverence that Jews would not pronounce it, and eventually the vowels were forgotten. God was known from the creation by His personal, self-designated covenantal name (Gen. 4:1), and the significance of that name was further enhanced by the Exodus. God was known as the One who makes covenants and even more as the One who keeps and fulfills His covenants (Ex. 6:3-8).

The addition of ṣᵉbā᾽ôt further emphasizes His divine sovereignty. The title has military overtones, inasmuch as Jehovah is the true head of Israel's (and the kingdom of God's) armies and of the hosts of heaven (1 Sam. 17:45). Furthermore, He is not just head of the hosts but King over all the world (Ps. 24:9; Isa. 37:16; Zech. 14:16). The time will come when all the universe will bow before its sovereign King, the Lord of hosts (Isa. 13:4; 24:21; 29:5-8; etc.). Even now He rules over all things, making them conform to His will (Ps. 80:19; Amos 4:13; 5:8; 9:5).

NASB, NKJV, RSV: Lord of hosts
NIV: Lord Almighty
LB: Lord of Hosts

M

85
mercyseat (Heb. 9:5)
  GREEK: *hilastērion*

Although the Greek word occurs twice in the New Testament (Rom. 3:25; Heb. 9:5), it is translated "mercyseat" only in Heb 9:5. The neuter substantive is formed from *hilastērios*, which does not occur as such in the New Testament. Another related term, *hilasmos* ("expiation, propitiation"), occurs in the well-known passages 1 John 2:2 and 4:10. Why, then, is *hilastērion* often translated "mercyseat" in Heb 9:5? The answer begins in the use of the term in the Septuagint (Greek Old Testament) to translate two different Hebrew words. Sometimes it was used to represent the Hebrew *kappōret*, which is derived from the common verb and noun *kāpar* ("make atonement, reconciliation"). The term always refers to the gold-covered lid, or top, of the Ark of the Covenant and is mentioned in Ex. 25:17, 18, 19, 20 (twice), 21, 22; 26:34; 30:6; 31:7; 35:12; 37:6, 7, 8, 9 (twice); 39:35; 40:20; and Lev 16:2, 13, 14 (twice), 15; cf. Num. 7:89. However, in three passages in Exodus (26:34; 30:6; 40:20) and in 1 Chron. 28:11, the Septuagint uses another Greek term for *kappōret*.

The Latin Vulgate translates *hilastērion* in Heb. 9:5 as *propitiatorium*, which was followed by Wycliffe (1380): "on which things were chembyus of glorie over schadowynge the propiciatorie." But Tyndale (1526) did not follow the Vulgate or the Septuagint, which lay behind it, but turned to Martin Luther's German translation of 1522 and rendered Hebrews 9:5 as "Over the arcke were the cherbis of glory shadowynge the seate of grace." From Tyndale, "mercyseat" was introduced into the KJV in 1611. The Romance language versions (French, Italian, Spanish, etc.) retain the *propitiatia* of the Latin, and from this Vulgate usage the word entered the English language.

The importance to biblical theology of the covering of the Ark of the Covenant is that it was the site of the holiest of all Jewish Old Testament rituals—the place where once each year the high priest entered into the Most Holy Place (Holy of Holies) and sprinkled the blood of the sacrifice. On that place and time was the focus of redemption, the prefigurement of Christ's sacrificial atonement for the sins of His people.

The versions cited all read "mercy seat," except the NIV, which reads, "the place of atonement."

86
Maranatha (1 Cor. 16:22)
  ARAMAIC: *māran'ātā'*
  GREEK: *marana tha*

    The phrase is an English transliteration of a Greek transliteration of the Aramaic, and appears only in 1 Cor. 16:22, in Paul's closing salutation. The Greek consists of a proper noun with pronominal suffix (*marana*, "Lord-our") and the verb *tha* ("come"). Although there is some question as to the exact force of the verb, the best explanation is that it is imperative—making the phrase a very short prayer in the form of an exhortation for Christ's soon return. A similar Greek expression is used in Rev 22:20, and there is a likelihood that the phrase in its Aramaic form passed into the liturgy of the early church. In a document called the Didache, or "The Teaching of the Lord by the Twelve Apostles to the Gentiles" (early second century), "Maranatha" appears in the celebration of the Lord's Supper. If this was a common usage in the early church, then it would have passed over intact without translation to the other languages of the early Christians and, like "amen," have been readily understood.

    Three aspects of this prayer are worth noting: (1) it calls directly upon Jesus Christ as Lord (*Mar*); (2) it holds the second coming to be foremost in the minds and hearts of believers and connects it to the Lord's Supper; and (3) it looks for, in fact beseeches, His immediate return.

  NASB: Maranatha
  NIV: Come, O Lord!
  NKJV: O Lord, come!
  RSV: Our Lord, come!
  LB: Lord Jesus, come!

87
with **Mary his espoused wife** (Luke 2:5)
  GREEK: *sun Mariam tēi emnēsteumenēi autōi*

    This phrase occurs only in Luke 2:5, although closely related phrases appear in Matt. 1:18 and Luke 1:27. It is a prepositional phrase introduced by *sun* ("with") followed by its object *Mariam* ("Mary"), modified by a participial phrase. The participial phrase opens with the definite article before the participle, which is further modified by the pronoun (genitive of indentification).

In New Testament times Jewish girls generally married quite young (at age 12 or 13). These marriages were contracted beforehand by the parents of the girl and of the prospective husband. The contract was solemnized by an oath (see Ezek. 16:8) and sealed with the payment of a "bride-price" (*mōhar*). The *mōhar* usually was a sum of money given to the girl's father (sometimes part of it was given to the bride, who wore it as jewelry). This was not to pay for the bride but to reimburse the family for the girl's economic worth to the family in a society where most families worked in cottage industries. The bride's father was to hold it in trust in case of a divorce or of the husband's death. While holding it in trust he could invest but not spend it, because to lose it might deprive his daughter and her children. In Jesus' day the two families met in front of a witness while the man gave the girl a token or a written document promising to marry her. He said, "By this ring [or token, document, etc.] you are set apart for me according to the Law of Moses and Israel."

Such espousal or betrothal was formal and binding, falling somewhere between present day engagement and marriage. During this stage neither party was free to seek another marital commitment, and to break off an espousal was to forfeit the *mōhar*. Sexual relations with someone else's espoused was a form of adultery, and the guilty party was to be stoned (Deut. 22:23-24). A betrothed girl enjoyed the legal privileges of a wife (Judg. 14:15; 15:1), although she was to remain a virgin until the marriage ceremony (Gen. 19:14). There may, however, have been some alteration in the latter custom through the centuries.

NASB: Mary, who was engaged to him
NIV: Mary, who was pledged to be married to him
NKJV: Mary, his betrothed wife
RSV: Mary, his betrothed
LB: Mary, his fiancee

88
men of renown (Gen. 6:4)
HEBREW: 'anshê hashshēm

This phrase appears only in Gen. 6:4 and Num. 16:2, although near equivalents occur in 1 Chron. 5:24; 12:31. It consists of the plural construct noun, the plural of *'îsh*, followed by the noun *shēm* with a definite article appended (lit., "men of the name"). The word for "men" represents men as the counterpart of women, that is, males. *Shēm* ordinarily means "name," but may also refer to reputation, as in "let us make us a name" (Gen. 11:4) or making someone's name great (Gen. 12:2; 2 Sam. 7:9). Thus "men of the name" are men of great reputation, specifically in war and authority.

NASB, NIV, NKJV, RSV: men of renown
LB: of whom so many legends are told (cf. note)

89
my beloved Son (Matt. 3:17)
GREEK: *ho huios mou ho agapētos*

This phrase occurs seven times in the New Testament, the first time in Matt. 3:17. It appears in each of the synoptic accounts of the baptism and transfiguration and in Peter's reference to these events (2 Pet. 1:17). The phrase is made emphatic by the two definite articles. The noun *huios* ("son") dominates the phrase and is modified by *agapētos* ("beloved"), a verbal adjective. The adjective bears the overtones of its root verb, *agapaō*, which refers to loving that is deep-seated, thorough-going, intelligent (thought out), and purposeful (intentionally directed), and that stems from the entire personality. God's love for His only begotten Son is as great as God's heart, eternal and unlimited by time, and is based on His esteem for its object (Jesus Christ).

The enunciation of this phrase at Jesus' baptism (Matt. 3:17 and parallels) is often viewed as a formula of identification—God's declaration of Jesus' eternal sonship and the special place Jesus holds in His heart. It may also be viewed against the Old Testament background of king ideology. An Israelite king was God's son (adopted) and was declared to be so upon his coronation (1 Sam. 7:14; Ps. 2:7). It may be that at Jesus' baptism God was declaring Jesus to be both Son and messianic king. The transfiguration declaration holds the same two possibilities, although the majestic unveiling of divine glory suggests that the emphasis there is on Christ's eternal ontological sonship (Matt. 17:5 and parallels).

NASB: This is My beloved Son, in whom I am well-pleased
NIV: This is my Son, whom I love; with him I am well pleased
NKJV: This is My beloved Son, in whom I am well pleased
RSV: This is my beloved Son, with whom I am well pleased
LB: This is my beloved Son, and I am wonderfully pleased with him

90
My God, my God, why hast thou forsaken me? (Mark 15:34)
ARAMAIC: *elōi, elōi, lama sabachthani*
GREEK: *ho theos mou ho theos mou, eis ti egkatelipes me*

The cry of Jesus from the cross occurs in this form only in Mark 15:34, although an equivalent is in Matt. 27:46. It consists of two nouns with the personal pronoun appended, the particle for "why," and a simple verb. In the Greek translation, definite articles (*ho*) precede and emphasize the nouns, which are modified by the first person singular pronoun (genitive of description). The verb *egkatelipes* is in the aorist tense and indicative mood. The interrogative phrase *eis ti* means "why?" or "for what purpose?" The question is an Aramaic citation of Ps. 22:1.

In crucial and deeply personal times Jesus often spoke in Aramaic, the language of the common people. Here Jesus unveils His suffering as a truly human being. He recognized His love for the Father and the Father's love for Him ("My God, my God"). Yet in the terrible agony of the cross, He was driven to ask why all this was upon Him—even as He had prayed in Gethsemane (Matt. 26:39). A mystery that cannot be penetrated prevents us from fully understanding the significance of Jesus' cry. He did not challenge His Father's wisdom or love, but was expressing His deep agony in becoming sin in behalf of lost mankind.

NASB, RSV: "Eloi, Eloi, lama sabachthani?" ... "My God, My God, why hast Thou forsaken Me?"

NIV, NKJV: "Eloi, Eloi, lama sabachthani?" ... "My God, my God, why have you forsaken me?"

LB: Eli, Eli, lama sabachthani? ("My God, my God, why have you deserted me?")

91
my redeemer liveth (Job 19:25)
HEBREW: *gō'ălī ḥāy*

This clause occurs only in Job 19:25 and consists of a singular noun (actually a participle with an affixed first-person personal pronoun), followed by the adjective *ḥāy* (nonpausal). The root *gā'al* refers to: (1) the responsibility of a kinsman to redeem (buy back) a poor man's person, family, or property from indenture arising out of poverty (Lev. 25:25) or warfare, (2) a person's privilege of redeeming a person or thing dedicated to the Lord (Lev. 27:11), (3) the responsibility to take the life of anyone who murders a kinsman (Num. 35:12), (4) the responsibility of the nearest kinsman to bear a son through the widow of his deceased and childless relative (see Ruth 3:13), and (5) the act of God by which He vindicates and redeems (reestablishes in peace and prosperity) His people (Isa. 43:1-3).

Much debate has centered on the use of *gōʾēl* in Job 19:25. The context makes clear that Job's hope and comfort was that away from or outside his flesh he would see God (v. 26). This parallels "at the last He will take His stand on the earth" (v. 25). He wishes his words were engraved on rock and inscribed in iron that they might last until the day when everything will be set straight—when His Redeemer-God will take his part, plead his case, and establish his vindication (vv. 23-24). Isaiah used and expanded this same concept of a Redeemer-God who will vindicate His people (Isa. 41:14; 43:14; 44:6, 24; 47:4; 48:17; 49:7, 26; 54:5; 60:16; 63:16), as does the psalmist (Pss. 19:14; 78:35). The appellation is used in close conjunction with "Savior" in passages such as Isa. 60:16. Who can deny Jesus is the Savior and Redeemer-Vindicator of His people, who will stand upon the earth in the end of days?

All the versions cited read "I know that my Redeemer lives" (RSV note: Or "Vindicator")

N

the **napkin, that was about his head** (John 20:7)
GREEK: *to soudarion, ho hēn epi tēs kephalēs autou*

This phrase describes the head wrapping used on Lazarus (John 11:44) and Jesus (John 20:7). The Greek uses the noun *soudarion*, borrowed from the Latin *sudarium* ("face cloth" or "handkerchief"). Such a cloth was used to tie up the jaw of a dead person. It was wound from the top of the head around the sides and under the chin to keep the mouth closed until burial. Although the grammar is not complicated, translators have had difficulty with the phrase. It consists of the noun *soudarion* with the definite article *to*, followed by a relative clause. This clause consists of the relative pronoun *ho* ("that"), followed by the third person singular of the past tense of the verb *hēn* ("was"). Then comes a genitive construction with the definite article feminine singular to conform to the noun *kephalēs* ("head"), followed by the masculine singular pronoun *autou* ("his").

The translation of Wycliffe (1380) follows the Latin *sudarium* directly, and reads "and the sudarie that was on his heed." The word *napkin* was first introduced in Tyndale's version of 1534. John's gospel states that the cloth was undisturbed when the disciples investigated the tomb. This fact is significant because it shows that the body had not been stolen in its wrappings, nor had Jesus simply recovered consciousness after fainting. An extraordinary and miraculous event had taken place. Contemporary versions vary considerably in their renderings.

NASB: and the face-cloth which had been on His head
NIV: as well as the burial cloth that had been around Jesus' head
NKJV: and the handkerchief that had been around His head
RSV: and the napkin, which had been on his head
LB: while the swath that had covered Jesus' head

93

no form nor comeliness (Isa. 53:2)
HEBREW: *lō-tō'ar lô wᵉlō' hādār*

This phrase appears only in Isa. 53:2 and consists of the negative particle *lō* ("no"), followed by a noun and a prepositional phrase, after which is another negative particle followed by the noun *hādār*. The term *tō'ar* relates to form or figure rather than appearance (see Gen. 29:17). Isaiah remarks that the Servant's form would be so marred and disfigured (52:14) that He would be repulsive to look at (53:2). *Hādār* represents the attribute in a king (or person) that elicits respect. The verbal root carries the idea of showing respect to one's elders or treating even the socially inferior with the respect due them as God's image-bearers. Descriptive of a king, the noun represents both the *attribute* worthy of royalty or majesty (Ps. 21:5; 45:3-4) and the *actions* worthy of such a one (Dan. 4:34). The Servant will have no form befitting an emissary (Servant) of the Lord and no personality that attracts a following. Neither His outward form nor His inward disposition, of themselves, would command a following among men.

NASB: He has no stately form or majesty
NIV: He had no beauty or majesty
NKJV, RSV: He has (had) no form or comeliness
LB: there was no attractiveness at all

O

94
our daily bread (Matt. 6:11)
GREEK: *ton arton hēmōn ton epiousion*

This well-known phrase from the Lord's Prayer appears only in the accounts of Matthew (6:11) and Luke (11:3). The three-word English phrase of the KJV represents a five-word Greek phrase in the original. Although four of the words are common in Greek of all periods, one has never been found in any other ancient literature. The term *arton*, with its definite article, simply means "bread," and the pronoun *hēmōn* ("our") and the following definite article are simple and straightforward. But *epiousion* has troubled scholars for centuries. Many attempts have been made to find the basic meaning of the word through its etymology or by determining the Aramaic term that Jesus actually spoke. Neither effort has been very successful, and ancient translations only confuse the issue. The Latin Vulgate, following Origen, reads *panem nostrum supersubstantialem* ("our supersubstantial bread") in Matt. 6:11, but *panem nostrum quotidianum* ("our daily bread") in Luke 11:3. The Syriac reads "bread of our continual need." But it has been universally agreed throughout the history of the church that the sense of the term is "day by day," that is, regular and dependable divine provision. This aspect of God's care for His people is mentioned frequently in the Old Testament (e.g., Job 23:12; Prov. 30:8-9; Ezek. 16:27). The provision of such food was also a royal responsibility (see Jer. 37:21; 2 Kings 25:29-30; Dan. 1:5).

NASB, NIV, NKJV, RSV: our daily bread
LB: our food again today, as usual

E.M. Yamauchi, "The Daily Bread Motif in Antiquity," *The Westminster Theological Journal* 28, no. 2 (May 1966): 145-56.

95
only begotten Son (John 3:16)
GREEK: *ton huion ton monogenē*

A key occurrence of this phrase is in John 3:16. It consists of the noun *huion* preceded by the definite article and *monogenē*, a noun which modifies the first noun. The second noun is made emphatic by the definite article before it. In fact, the two definite articles make the entire phrase emphatic. In the book of Hebrews *monogenē* is used of Isaac, Abraham's "only begotten son" (11:17). But in John the meaning is enriched by reference to Jesus the Word as "the only begotten of the Father" (John 1:14). The phrase focuses on Christ's eternal, trinitarian, and ontological sonship (John 1:1, 18). He was sent into the world by the Father in order that the world might be saved through Him (John 3:16-17; 1 John 4:9). Used of Jesus, *monogenē* speaks of the eternal generation (begetting) of the Son of God. He is God's own Son (Rom. 8:32), the eternal Son (John 17:5, 24; Heb. 1:5; 5:5), who has been given life in Himself (John 5:26). He is the only begotten Son of God (John 1:18) and is equal to the Father in knowledge (Matt. 11:27; Luke 10:22) and work (John 10:30).

NASB: only begotten Son
NIV: one and only Son (note: Or, "his only begotten Son")
NKJV: only begotten Son
RSV: only Son
LB: only Son (note: Or, "the unique Son of God")

96

the **order of Melchisedec** (Heb. 7:17)
GREEK: *kata tēn taxin Melchisedek*

This phrase in Heb. 7:17 (see also 5:6, 10; 6:20; 7:11, 21) finds its original meaning in the Old Testament. It is a prepositional phrase introduced by *kata* ("according to"), followed by the definite article *tēn* and the noun *taxin* ("rank" or "order"), modified by the proper name *Melchisedek* ("Melchisedec" or "Melchizedek"), who appears without much explanation in Gen. 14:18-20. The name is really a title, "King of Righteousness," and we are not told his actual name. He was the priest-king of ancient Jerusalem who brought Abram bread and wine, who blessed him, and through whom Abram offered a tithe to God—of whom Melchizedek was a true representative. By this receiving and giving Abram publicly identified with Melchizedek spiritually and theologically.

In Ps. 110:4 God proclaims by an oath the coming Davidic king (the Messiah) as "a priest forever after the order of Melchizedek." The writer of Hebrews proclaims Jesus as the Messiah and the priest after the order of Melchizedek. He notes that both are kings of righteousness and of peace, both are without descent with reference to their office, and both are eternal priests—Melchizedek in the sense that the end of his office is not recorded and Christ in the sense that His office has no end. This order of priesthood is superior to that of Aaron because (1) Abram offered a tithe through Melchizedek (whereas the Aaronic/Levitical priesthood came much later and was, in fact, descended from Abram); (2) the psalmist prophesied that it was to replace Aaron's order; (3) God established it as greater by undergirding it with His own oath; and (4) unlike Aaron's order, Christ's is permanent (Heb. 7:4-25).

NASB, NIV, NKJV, RSV: the order of Melchizedek
LB: the rank of Melchizedek

97
out of great tribulation (Rev. 7:14)
GREEK: *ek tēs thlipseōs tēs megalēs*

This phrase appears only in Rev. 7:14, although many see related references elsewhere in the Bible. The noun *thlipseōs* is preceded by the definite article, as is the adjective *megalēs* ("great"). Following a preposition, a definite article is not needed to make a noun definitive, and this construction therefore refers to a particular tribulation already known to the readers. *Thlipsis* means a "pressing together" or "squeezing," as of grapes, or used figuratively, a distress or tribulation. The Great Tribulation is linked to Dan. 12:1 by Jesus in the Olivet discourse (Matt 24:21; Mark 13:19, 24; Luke 21:20-24). There is much disagreement as to the time of the Great Tribulation. Equally sincere and godly Christians place it before or after Christ's second coming. Some urge that this phrase in Rev. 7:14 refers specifically to the destruction of Jerusalem in 70 A.D., and in general to all that happens to the church prior to Christ's second coming (Acts 7:11). Others hold that it is a seven-year period after Christ's return, but before He begins the Millennium.

The versions cited all read "out of the Great Tribulation."

P

98

maketh his son or his daughter to **pass through the fire** (Deut. 18:10)
HEBREW: *ma‘ăbîr bᵉnô-ûbittô bā’ēsh*

This phrase first appears in Deut. 18:10, although the verb by itself, and carrying the technical meaning, appears in Lev. 18:21. The first word of the phrase is a causative participle and is followed by two direct objects (both singular), joined by a simple conjunction ("or") and a prepositional phrase modifying the verbal idea. The full phrase (with the verb in participial or other moods) appears six times in the Old Testament, while the abbreviated form (verb without the prepositional phrase) appears four times.

The ancient Canaanites viewed the act of burning children, usually infants, in fire as a supreme sacrifice. This act, strictly forbidden in the Mosaic law (Lev. 18:21; Deut. 18:19), was associated with soothsaying or trying to discern and control the future, or even to totally control all of life. Much archaeological evidence of the practice exists outside of Israel, especially among the Phoenicians (northern Canaanites). It was introduced into Israel by Solomon (1 Kings 11:7, 33) but did not gain widespread acceptance until the time of Ahaz (2 Kings 16:3). Such sacrifices were made to the pagan god Molech and, after cremation, the victims' remains were placed in urns. In Israel such rites occurred in the valley of Hinnom at a site known as Topheth. Josiah polluted this site in order to discontinue the practice. The act itself is mentioned in the NASB, but the LB, RSV, and NIV also indicate its significance.

NASB, NKJV: makes his son or (his) daughter pass through the fire
NIV: sacrifices his son or daughter in the fire (note: Or, "who makes his son or daughter pass through")
RSV: burns his son or his daughter as an offering (note: Or, "makes his son or his daughter pass through the fire")
LB: presents his child to be burned to death as a sacrifice (note: "Implied")

J.I. Packer, M.C. Tenney, W. White, Jr., eds., "Ugarit and the Canaanites," in *The Bible Almanac* (Nashville: Nelson, 1980), pp. 138-47.

99

the **peace of God** (Phil. 4:7)
  GREEK: *hē eirēnē tou theou*

This phrase, occurring as such only in Phil. 4:7, consists of the definite article, the noun *eirēnē*, another definite article (genitive of description) and its noun, *theou* (genitive of description). In this passage Paul states that the divine peace will guard believers. It is a peace related to the salvation of the whole man, and comes from the "God of peace" (Phil. 4:9; cf. Rom. 15:33; 1 Thess. 5:23). According to Jesus, salvation consists of the things that make for peace (Luke 19:42), and He pronounced such peace upon all believers in Him (John 14:27; 16:33). Salvation, therefore, is the "good news of peace by Jesus Christ" (Acts 10:36), the preaching of peace (Eph. 2:17), and the "gospel of peace" (Eph. 6:15; cf. Rom 10:15).

These ideas continue the Old Testament description of peace as an eschatological reality, centering primarily on spiritual blessings (Isa. 54:10; Jer. 29:11; Ezek. 34:25), although not excluding temporal blessings. This was the comprehensive peace associated with life in the phrase "covenant of life and peace" (Mal. 2:5). Thus true peace can remain even when material evidence of it does not (Isa. 48:18; 57:2; 59:8; 60:17). Eschatological peace is described further in terms of the restoration of paradise (Isa. 11:6-9; Hos. 2:20; Amos 9:13) and the establishing of the kingdom of God (Isa. 2:2; Mic. 4:3) under and through the Messiah (Isa. 9:6, 7; Mic. 5:2-5; Zech. 9:9). This is the peace Jesus brought, which believers have in Him (Rom. 5:1, 10; Eph. 2:14-17) and which comes only by grace (2 Pet. 3:14). It is a product of the salvation of the whole man, experienced by the believer as God's eternal power (Phil. 4:7; Col. 3:15).

  NASB, NIV, NKJV, RSV: peace of God
  LB: God's peace

100

pinnacle of the temple (Matt. 4:5)
  GREEK: *pterugion tou hierou*

This phrase describes the elevation where Jesus was taken by Satan to be tempted, as described in Matt 4:5 and Luke 4:9. The phrase consists of the rare term *pterugion*, the diminutive of the common Greek term for "wing," which also denoted the summit or apex of something. The other noun in the phrase is the common Greek term for "temple." The best rendering of the phrase is therefore "the highest point of the Temple."

The temple referred to is the one begun by Herod in 20 B.C. and destroyed in the Roman destruction of Jerusalem in A.D. 70. In the last several decades Israeli archaeologists have excavated the western and southern walls of Herod's temple, and some of the blocks and inscriptions from the highest point on the southern tower have been found. The letters of the inscription are in monumental round script, marking the place where the trumpeters stood.

NASB, NKJV, RSV: the pinnacle of the temple
NIV: the highest point of the temple
LB: the roof of the Temple

101
potter's field (Matt. 27:7)
GREEK: *agron tou kerameōs*

This phrase occurs only in Matt. 27:7, 10. It consists of the masculine noun *agron* modified by the noun *kerameōs* (genitive of identification), which is made definite by the article *tou*. *Agron* means a field, a plot of ground used mainly for agriculture. Apparently this field, or at least its owner, was well known, and it was purchased with Judas's blood money as a burial place for strangers (Matt. 27:7). It was renamed, consequently, as "the field of blood" (Greek *agros haimatos*, Matt. 27:8; Aramaic *akeldama*, cf. Acts 1:19).

According to tradition, this graveyard is located south of Jerusalem in the Valley of Hinnom, west of its junction with the Valley of Kidron. The field contains some first-century tombs and clay suitable for the manufacture of pottery.

NASB: the Potter's Field
NIV, NKJV, RSV: the potter's field
LB: a certain field where the clay was used by potters

B. Van Elderen, "Akeldama," in *Zondervan Pictorial Encyclopedia of the Bible* (Grand Rapids: Zondervan, 1976), 1:94.

102
And it was the **preparation of the passover** (John 19:14)
GREEK: *ēn de paraskeuē tou pascha*

This phrase, appearing only in John 19:14, consists of the verb ēn (aorist indicative), the postpositive particle *de* (indicating a somewhat stronger conjunction than *kai*), the feminine noun *paraskeue* (nominative singular), and the definite article *tou* modifying the second noun, *pascha*. The phrase is properly rendered "the preparation of the Passover," rather than "preparation for the Passover." Jesus was sentenced on the day of the Passover, that is, Friday of Passover week. So Luke says, "And that day was the preparation, and the sabbath drew on" (23:54), while Mark has, "It was the preparation, that is, the day before the sabbath" (15:42). This was the day (before sunset on Friday) on which Jews prepared for the Sabbath by suspending usual business and social activities and preparing all food in advance.

NASB: Now it was the day of preparation for the Passover
NIV: It was the day of Preparation of Passover Week
NKJV: Now it was the Preparation Day of the Passover
RSV: Now it was the day of Preparation of the Passover
LB: It was now about noon of the day before Passover

103
the **publicans and the harlots** (Matt. 21:32)
GREEK: *hoi de telōnai kai hai pornai*

This phrase, first appearing in Matt. 21:32, consists of two nouns, each modified by their definite articles and joined by the conjunction *kai*. The first noun is best rendered "tax collectors." In ancient Rome the government often sold the privilege of collecting taxes. Rich men, usually foreigners living in the lands to be taxed, would buy the privilege. Apparently Zacchaeus, though himself a Jew, had purchased this privilege. He is called an *architelōnēs*, a chief or head tax collector (Luke 19:2), in Latin called *publicani* ("publicans"). Those men then hired local citizens (who became *telōnai*) to do the actual collecting.

The many and varied Roman taxes included: (1) a poll tax paid by every adult male over fourteen and every female over twelve, except the aged; (2) a land tax; and (3) export-import taxes.

Tax collectors were visible and ever-present reminders of the hated foreign domination. They often overcharged and pocketed the excess. They were hated intensely and looked down upon as the lowest kind of people, often being ranked with prostitutes—as in this phrase.

Widespread from very ancient days (Gen. 34:31), prostitution was strongly prohibited in the Mosaic law (Lev. 19:29; Deut. 22:21) and the book of Proverbs (7:16-27). Harlots were clearly recognizable, perhaps by the way they braided their hair and wore jewelry (cf. Ezek. 16:10-

13), as some ancient Near Eastern figures suggest. They also usually seem to have been veiled (Gen. 38:14-15). In all periods, pagan worship often included the practice of paid sexual cohabitation. Women engaging in such activities were known as "priestesses" or "dedicated ones" (Hebrew *q^edēshâ*).

In the New Testament period it seems that prostitution continued to be widespread. Both tax collectors and prostitutes were ritually unclean by Jewish law or tradition and would render all who associated with them unclean. Pious Jews, therefore, avoided all unnecessary contact with them. Even such outcasts as tax collectors and prostitutes, however, were ministered to (Matt. 9:11) and redeemed (John 4:14) by Christ. His mission was to sinners (Matt. 9:13).

NASB: the tax-gatherers and harlots
NIV: the tax collectors and the prostitutes
NKJV, RSV: the tax collectors and the harlots
LB: very evil men and prostitutes

W. White, Jr., "Finances," in S. Benko and J.J. O'Rourke, eds., *The Catacombs and the Colosseum* (Philadelphia: Judson, 1971), pp. 218-36.

R

104
Rabboni (John 20:16)
GREEK: *rhabbouni*

This transliteration of the Greek (which is itself a transliteration of the Aramaic) appears only in Mark 10:51 and John 20:16. Literally, and according to its form, this word is a type of address, since it consists of the noun with an affixed second person singular pronoun and means "my lord" or "my master." Apparently the word became a title, which was given only to the most respected teachers and to God. It was a title of the highest respect, equivalent perhaps to "doctor" in modern society. Unlike "doctor," however, this title was attached to a person by his followers. John the Baptist's followers called him "rabbi" (a shortened form of the word).

It is noteworthy that at the outset of His public ministry, Jesus' followers called Him "rabbi," while the crowds called Him the Greek *kurios* (in the broad meaning of "sir"). Later the crowds also called Him "rabbi," and the disciples called Him *rabbi* and *kurios* after the discourse on the bread of life (John 6:68). The disciples, however, used *kurios* in its more narrow sense of "Lord." The title *rabboni* was used of Jesus by blind Bartimaeus (Mark 10:51), and Mary Magdalene used it of Christ with the deepest respect and reverence. After the resurrection Jesus is referred to only as *kurios,* and that perhaps in all its richness as a substitution for the divine name Jehovah, or Yahweh. His was "the name which is above every name" (Phil. 2:9; cf. Rev. 19:12).

All the versions cited read "Rabboni," except the LB, which has "Master."

105
Rahab and Babylon (Ps. 87:4)
HEBREW: *rahab ûbābel*

This phrase occurs in the middle verse of a short but difficult psalm. It is a unique phrase, used in a rare triple-level parallel construction. The psalm deals with the kingdom of Jehovah and sets the holy hill of

Zion as the center of the kingdoms of the world. A time is foreseen when all of Israel's traditional enemies will be considered citizens of Zion. The three lines of the psalm in literal translation are:

I will declare Rahab and Babel to know Me,
Behold, Philistia and Tyre with Cush,
"This one was born there."

From Isa. 30:7, a prophecy against Judah's alliance with Egypt, we learn that "Rahab" is a poetic name for that kingdom (this Rahab is not the woman of Josh. 2 or Matt. 1:5). Unfortunately the KJV mistranslates the name Rahab as the noun for "strength," but the verse properly reads "to Egypt, whose help is utterly useless. Therefore I call her Rahab the Do-Nothing" (NIV).

But how did the name Rahab come to refer to Egypt? It seems that Rahab was the name of a primordial dragon or sea monster that was conquered by God or one of His angels and was destroyed. Whether or not this is a literary reference to some ancient epic, which is very likely, has never been settled. Allusions to Rahab the sea monster are found in Ps. 89:10, "Thou hast broken Rahab in pieces"; Isa 51:9, "Art thou not he that both cut Rahab, and wounded the dragon?"; and twice in Job 9:13. But here again the KJV misread the text and has "the proud helpers do stoop under him." A more accurate translation is "even the cohorts of Rahab cowered at his feet" (NIV). So then Rahab was a monster of the seas in ancient Semitic epics, and the name was applied to Egypt in later literature such as the Psalms. The pair of enemies in the first line of Ps. 87:4 are Egypt and Babel (or Babylon). The list of three enemies—Philistia, Tyre, and Cush (or Sudan)—are parallel to the first pair. The third line is a short colloquial snatch of everyday conversation indicating that the citizens of the many nations are now citizens of holy Zion. A more understandable paraphrase of the passage is: "I will include Egypt and Babylonia when I list the nations that obey me; the people of Philistia, Tyre and Sudan I will number among the inhabitants of Jerusalem" (*Good News Bible*).

All the cited versions read "Rahab and Babylon," except LB, which has "Egypt and Babylonia."

106
rent his clothes (Judg. 11:35)
  HEBREW: *wayyiqra' et-b°gādāw*

This phrase consists of the verb *qāra'* ("to tear," imperfect, third masculine singular), followed by *et*, the sign of the direct object, and the plural noun *bᵉgādāw* ("garment"). The phrase signifies the expression of the deepest, heartfelt grief, in which the ancients of many cultures would tear the upper and under garments covering their chests so as to expose the area over their hearts. The news of Joseph's supposed death thrust Jacob into the throes of grief and led him to tear his garments (Gen. 37:34). Rending the garments was often accompanied by the donning of sackcloth (Gen. 37:34), throwing ashes or dirt on one's head (1 Sam. 4:12), and removing one's shoes and covering one's head with his hands (2 Sam. 15:30). God promises to rend the hearts of those who refuse to show proper contrition for their sin (Hos. 13:8), and calls on His sinful people to rend their own hearts, rather than simply their garments (Joel 2:13).

NASB, NIV, NKJV, LB: he tore his clothes
RSV: he rent his clothes

107
rewards of divination (Num. 22:7)
  HEBREW: *ûqsāmîm*

This phrase occurs only in Num. 22:7, although similar Hebrew forms appear in Deut. 18:10 and 2 Kings 17:17. Normally *qesem* denotes a variety of divination, probably practiced by shaking or throwing arrows down, consulting images (teraphim), hepatoscopy ("reading" a liver), and perhaps telling the future by "reading" arrows (see Ezek. 21-22). The context in Num. 22:7 shows that this word is used elliptically for the fee or reward Balak's emissaries were carrying in their hands for Balaam's work—conceived as any variety of means by which he would tell the future, and even control the future, to assure that Israel would be cursed and lose the battle. In their second try to hire Balaam, when Balak's servants reported how much he could reward Balaam, the seer replied that, though Balak give him his house full of silver and gold, he could not do what the king wanted. The term, therefore, here clearly refers to the fee or payment for divination, not the divination itself.

NASB, RSV: the fees for divination
NIV: the fee for divination
NKJV: the diviner's fee
LB: with money in hand

108
ruler of the Jews (John 3:1)
   GREEK: *archōn tōn Ioudaiōn*

This phrase appears only in John 3:1 in identifying Nicodemus as the one who came to Jesus by night. He may have come secretly out of temerity because of his fellow Pharisees or out of the desire to get Jesus' full attention, or both. A ruler of the Jews was a member of the highest court of Judaism, the Sanhedrin. Elsewhere called the presbytery or court of elders (Luke 22:66; Acts 22:5), this body consisted of chief priests (former high priests), scribes (or teachers of the Pharisaical traditions), and elders (prominent lay leaders whose sympathies were with the Sadducees)—all of whom had to be wealthy and old before being admitted to the council of seventy.

In Jesus' day Rome allowed the Sanhedrin almost total control of the Jewish nation with regard to internal affairs. They managed religious, civil, and criminal matters usually without interference from the Roman governor, as long as taxes were paid and order was maintained. Nicodemus was a prominent scholar and teacher of rabbinic oral law (John 3:10). As a Pharisee he believed that Abrahamic lineage was crucial to entering the kingdom of God—as was perfect performance, in act and in spirit, of the whole law. At a later date Nicodemus hesitantly but successfully defended Jesus when He was being discussed during a meeting of the Sanhedrin (John 7:50-51). His faith apparently had come to full bloom by the time he helped Joseph of Arimathea obtain and properly bury Jesus' body (John 19:38-42).

NASB, NKJV, RSV: a ruler of the Jews
NIV: a member of the Jewish ruling council
LB: a Jewish religious leader

S

secret place of the most High (Ps. 91:1)
  HEBREW: *bᵉsēter ʿelyôn*

This phrase occurs only in Ps. 91:1 and opens with the preposition *bᵉ* prefixed to the singular construct noun *sēter*, followed by the proper name *ʿelyôn*. Elyon is a very ancient divine appellation, first appearing biblically in Gen. 14:18, where it modifies, or is an appositive of, *ʿEl* (another ancient name of God). Elyon appears to be a superlative of the root *ʿālāh* ("to go up"). As an adjective *ʿelyôn* refers to supremacy in position (Deut. 28:1) or to high location (Gen. 40:17). Significantly, Ps. 97:9 uses this word as a divine name or appellative, but in the same phrase that occurs in Deut. 28:1. In that passage Israel's obedience to God would make her supreme (*elyon*) over all the nations of the land (*ʿereṣ*). In Ps. 97 God is *ʿelyôn* (most high, supreme) over all the earth (*ʿereṣ*). *ʿElyôn*, therefore, basically means supreme.

It seems likely that this name by which God revealed Himself to Melchizedek (Gen. 14:18-20) is reflected, however dimly, in the Ugaritic literature. The Hebrew *sēter* means "place of shelter and protection." So in Ps. 27:5 the psalmist confesses that God hides him in the secret place of His tent—that is, hides him away in protection as an ancient nomad secreted and protected his women and children in the inner room of his tent. Similarly, God is the hiding place of protection (Ps. 32:7; 119:114). This explains why in Ps. 61:4 the psalmist takes refuge in the shelter (*sēter*) of God's wings, and why in 91:1 our phrase parallels "shadow of the Almighty." If the image is that of a powerful bird of prey feared by all, the psalmist is confessing that the most powerful and supreme God is his protector. All His fearsome power keeps the enemy away. Protection, rather than secrecy, is at the heart of this phrase.

NASB, NIV, RSV: in the shelter of the Most High
NKJV: secret place of the Most High
  LB: sheltered by the God who is above all gods

110
her **seed** (Gen. 3:15)
   HEBREW: *zar̆āh*

This Hebrew phrase occurs in the so-called *protevangelium* ("first declaration of the gospel"). It consists of a singular noun to which is affixed the feminine singular pronoun. As elsewhere in Semitic languages, the word for "seed" here means offspring or posterity. The noun is always collective (in the singular) when so used. In Gen. 3:15 it represents the spiritual descendants of Adam and Eve, those who would be under the covenant of redemption. Between them and the spiritual followers of Satan would be perpetual hostility. The human followers of Satan are also physical descendants ("seed") of Adam and Eve, the parents of all subsequent human beings.

This understanding of *zar̆āh* is further supported by Gen. 4-6, where subsequent history is depicted as proceeding along two tracks: that of the godly and that of the ungodly. When God chose Noah, and especially when He chose Abram, this separation theme came into prominence again. Abram's seed is *the* seed of the woman (Gen. 12:7). Later revelation narrows this seed to David (2 Sam. 7:12) and in particular to His greater son, the Messiah (Ps. 18:50). The New Testament explains that the seed of David (John 7:42; Rom. 1:3) and of Abraham (Rom. 4:13) really was one person, Jesus Christ—the true seed of the woman (Rev. 12:17). All who are truly under the covenant, or in Christ, whether they lived before or after Him, are also true seed (Gal. 3:16), because they are one with Him (1 Cor. 12:12; Heb. 11:39- 40).

NASB, NKJV, RSV: your seed and her seed (Seed)
NIV, LB: your offspring and hers

111
seller of purple (Acts 16:14)
   GREEK: *porphuropōlis*

The English phrase is a translation of one compound Greek word, which appears only in Acts 16:14. The two elements of the term are *porphur* and *pōlis*. The first element derives from *porphura*, which originally represented purple dye extracted from the murex mollusk, and then the purple woolen cloth dyed with the extract (Luke 16:19). *Pōlis* is derived from the verb *pōleō*, meaning "to sell." Thus Lydia was a seller of purple cloth.

The art of extracting this dye was very ancient, the Phoenicians being especially well known for the art. Indeed, the name _Phoenician_ is derived from another Greek word meaning purple. Some have even argued that Canaan means "the land of purple," from a Hurrian place-name. In biblical times this purple dye and the clothes colored with it were expensive and much in demand by the rich and important as a sign of status. Archaeology has demonstrated that Thyatira was a textile center especially involved in the dyeing of purple cloth.

NASB: a seller of purple fabrics
NIV: a dealer in purple cloth
NKJV: a seller of purple
RSV: a seller of purple goods
LB: a merchant of purple cloth

112
servant of the LORD / the LORD's servant (Isa. 42:19)
HEBREW: 'ebed yhwh

This phrase, or its equivalent, occurs frequently in its technical official sense, as especially in Isa. 40-66. Its appearance in Isa. 52:13 ("my servant") has a singular noun with the first person singular pronoun affixed. Worshipers of God are His servants (Gen. 26:24; Deut. 32:36; 2 Kings 9:7; Isa. 65:15; etc.). The prophets are frequently called God's servants, those who do His bidding (e.g., 2 Kings 9:7; 17:13; Jer. 7:25).

The servant in Isa. 40-66 is sometimes national Israel (as in 42:18-19) and sometimes spiritual Israel (as in 41:8-10). As national Israel, she is the descendant of Abraham, the covenantal people—even though she does not faithfully adhere to the covenant. As spiritual Israel she is the elect of God, consisting of all Israelites who are true to God, whom Isaiah calls "the remnant." But this true remnant, this true spiritual Israel, finds fullest expression in the Servant who has a mission to Israel (42:1-7; 49:1-9; 50:4-10; 52:13—53:12). Especially important, therefore, is the use of this phrase in reference to the Messiah.

The servant of the Lord, therefore, may be conceived as a composite entity, a pyramid—with national Israel for a base, spiritual Israel forming the middle, and the Messiah as the apex. It is clear from Isaiah 52:13—53:12 and from the New Testament use of this passage that Jesus Christ is the true messianic Servant of the Lord.

NASB, NIV, RSV: the servant of the Lord
NKJV: the Lord's servant

LB: the "Servant of the Lord"

E.J. Young, *Studies in Isaiah* (Grand Rapids: Eerdmans, 1954), pp. 127-41.

113
seven stars and Orion (Amos 5:8)
HEBREW: *kîmā ûksîl*

Names of constellations appear in four locations in poetical sections of the Old Testament (Job 9:9; 38:31, 32; Amos 5:8). In each of these passages the names are given in highly figurative contexts, indicating God's transcendent authority over nature and the cosmos. In no case can the ancient Semitic names be associated with specific astronomical phenomena with certainty, and most names in English translations are based on the Septuagint (Greek Old Testament). Job 9:9 reads: Who makes the *'āsh, kesîl,* and the *kîmā*—all three of which are difficult to translate. But we will look at their uses and the evidence for their meanings in the four verses in which they appear. For each verse the Hebrew of the Masoretic Text (MT), the Greek of the Septuagint (LXX), the Latin of the Vulgate (LV), and the English of the KJV are shown.

Job 9:9

MT	*'āsh*	*kesîl*	*kîma*
LXX	*pleiada*	*hesperon*	*arktouron*
LV	*Arcturum*	*Oriana*	*Hyadas*
KJV	Arcturus	Orion	pleiades

Job 38:31

MT		*kesîl*	*kîmā*
LXX		*Pleiados*	*Orion*
LV		*Pliadis*	*Arcturi*
KJV		Pleiades	Orion

Job 38:32

MT	*'ayish*		*mazzā(r)ôt*
LXX	*hesperon*		*mazouroth*
LV	*vesperum*		*luciferum*
KJV	Arcturus		Mazzaroth

Amos 5:8

MT		*kesîl*	*kîmā*
LXX		*metaskeuazon*	*ektrepon*
LV		*Arcturus*	*Orion*
KJV		seven stars	Orion

From this chart it can be seen that the versions shift between meanings, with little regard for the original language of the text. Several things become clear. The Hebrew of Job uses two variants of *'āsh,* and only the KJV is consistent in using Arcturus in both places. There is currently no certain etymology for this Hebrew term, but the brilliance of the star Arcturus, which is of the first magnitude, certainly makes it an attractive possibility.

The second Hebrew term, *k^esîl,* is rendered by the Septuagint three different ways in three passages. The Latin Vulgate and KJV continue the confusion. Since the Hebrew term is in the plural (*k^esîlêhem* in Isa 13:10), it probably means simply "constellation"—since the constellations and signs of the Zodiac were well known to all of the ancient cultures and were the subject of endless mythological stories. The Hebrew *kîmā* has been considered to be related to the Akkadian *kimtu* ("family") and thus to refer to the Pleiades or seven stars. A recent tablet from Ebla reinforces this etymology. It seems that in an ancient lexical list of Sumerian astral deities and their Canaanite equivalents, the Sumerian *mul-mul* (Pleiades) is shown to be *ka-ma-tu,* the Hebrew *kîmā.* There is also evidence that it was used as a place-name. Today only six of the seven stars are visible with the unaided eye. There is good documentary evidence, however, that in antiquity all seven were plainly visible.

The last Hebrew term to be considered is the plural form *mazzālot/ mazzārôt,* which offers no problem in form, since the interchange of *l* and *r* is well known in Semitic languages. The Akkadian cognate of this word, *maṣṣaru(m),* means "a watcher, a guard," and is frequent in the literature. In the only other passage where the Hebrew word appears (2 Kings 23:5), it may refer to the positions of the zodiacal signs, as in astrology. Unlike the religious cultures all about them, Israel practiced virtually no astrology, which was condemned by Scripture. From this review it appears that the best rendering of Amos 5:8 is "It is he who made the Pleiades and Orion," which is followed by contemporary versions.

NASB, NIV, NKJV, RSV: the Pleiades and Orion
LB: the Seven Stars and the constellation Orion

M. Dahood, in G. Pettinato, *The Archives of Ebla* (New York: Doubleday, 1981), pp. 302-3. See also H.N. Tur-Sinai, *The Book of Job* (Jerusalem: Hebrew U. Press, 1957), pp. 529-30.

114
without **shedding of blood is no remission** (Heb. 9:22)
GREEK: *kai chōris haimatekchusias ou ginetai aphesis*

This clause, occurring only in Heb. 9:22, consists of the simple conjunction *kai* ("and"), the preposition *chōris* ("without"), the noun *haimatekchusias* (which occurs only here in all of Greek literature), the negative particle *ou* ("not"), the verb *ginetai* (lit., "there becomes"), and the noun *aphesis* ("remission"). *Haimatekchusias* is a compound word, consisting of *haima* ("blood") and *ekchusis*, a noun formed from the verb *ekcheō* ("to shed," "to pour"). The doctrine here is clearly related to the Old Testament requirement of blood (animal) sacrifice for the atonement of sins (Lev. 17:11)—which was also reflected in various rabbinical statements, such as "Does not atonement come through the blood" (TB Yoma 5a) and "Surely atonement can be only with the blood" (TB Zwpahim 6a).

The writer of Hebrews summarizes the truth that, even under the Old Testament, without shedding of blood there was no forgiveness of sin. That this refers to more than mere ceremonial covering, cleansing, and remission is established by Heb. 9:23 and 10:18. It is equally certain that the author does not intend his readers to conclude that the Old Testament animal sacrifices in themselves expiated sin (Heb. 10:4). Even in Old Testament times, spiritual cleansing rested on the blood of Christ (Heb. 10:14; cf. 9:13-14).

NASB, NIV, RSV, LB: without (the) shedding of blood there is no forgiveness
NKJV: without shedding of blood there is no remission

115
slow of speech, and of a slow tongue (Ex. 4:10)
HEBREW: *kᵉbad-peh ûkbad lāshôn*

This phrase occurs only in Ex. 4:10 and consists of a noun in the construct relationship followed by a noun in the absolute. Moses was protesting that he could not speak properly to Pharaoh as God's representative, since he was not skillful in using words. He was, literally, "heavy (*kᵉbad*) of mouth (*peh*) and heavy of tongue (*lāshôn*)." Perhaps the first condition refers to the mechanics of speech and the second to the flow of speech. If this is true, Moses protested that he had trouble getting words out and that those he did get out were inadequate. God responded that He would teach Moses how to speak (v. 11) and what to say (v. 12). Eventually, God appointed Aaron, Moses' brother, to be his "mouth," that is his spokesman, but the message was given to Moses (v. 15).

In this account we learn that (1) when God commands us to do something no excuse is adequate (since the canon of Scripture is closed we hear no voices from heaven, but the Bible is replete with still-valid divine commands); (2) with every command God gives enablement to accomplish it; and (3) God evaluates our abilities more accurately and objectively than we do.

NASB, NIV, NKJV, RSV: slow of speech and slow of tongue
LB: speech impediment

116
sons of God (Gen. 6:2)
HEBREW: $b^e n\hat{e}$-$h\bar{a}^{\cdot}\bar{e}l\bar{o}him$

This phrase is found in the beginning of the narrative of Noah and the Flood as well as in other passages and contexts, such as Job 1:5; 2:1; 38:7; and less specifically in Ps. 29:1. The Ugaritic phrase *bn'lm* is not cognate to this phrase in Gen 6:2 but is cognate to Hebrew $b^e n\hat{e}^{\cdot}\bar{e}lim$, as in Ex. 15:11; Ps. 29:1; and 89:6 [H v. 7]—in all of which passages it means "mighty one" or "mighty ones." A similar phrase is found in Dan 3:25 (in Aramaic) and in an incantation from Arslan Tash. In each of these cases the subjects are angels or other heavenly beings.

There are two major views on the phrase in Gen. 6:2. One is that the "sons of God" refers to superhuman or angelic beings—possibly even fallen angels, as in the myths of Babylon, where "the assembly of the gods" plays a part in the creation. The view continues to assert that the cohabitation of these beings with women produced the race of giants ($n^e phil\hat{i}m$) mentioned in v. 4.

The argument that these were simply the sons of the godly line of Seth (Gen. 5:6) is based on the following five points:

1. Although in the Job passages angelic beings are mentioned, there is no suggestion that they "came down" or were involved on earth in human affairs.
2. Gen. 6:2 clearly states that the "sons of God" took the "daughters of men" as wives, not merely temporary partners. They therefore must have been able to marry and settle down together.
3. These "sons of God" found the "daughters of men" desirable, and mated and produced children with them (v.4), which would have been possible only for human beings.
4. Jesus taught that angels do not marry (Matt. 22:30).
5. The Nephilim are not described anywhere in the Old Testament as being more than "giants," that is, simply very large men.

For the most detailed exposition of this viewpoint, see *The Companion Bible* (reprint, Grand Rapids: Zondervan, 1964), apps. 23, 25. See the further discussion in G. Vos, *Biblical Theology* (Grand Rapids: Eerdmans,

1954), pp. 58ff. This interpretation is also supported by the Judaeo-Arabic version of Saadia Ben Josef Al-Fayyoumi.

The versions cited all read "sons of God," except LB, which has "beings from the spirit world."

117
Son of man (Matt. 8:20)
GREEK: *huios tou anthrōpou*

This self-designation of Jesus consists of the noun *huios* ("son") modified by the noun *anthrōpou* ("man"), made definite by the article *tou* (both noun and article are genitive of identification). Some have seen in this phrase no more than an emphasis on the humanity of Jesus, comparing it to Old Testament counterparts in such passages as Ezek. 2:1-3, where it simply means a physical descendant of Adam, a human being. It is more likely, however, that on Jesus' lips (and throughout the gospels) the phrase reflects Dan. 7:13, where the "Son of man" is one to whom is given universal and eternal authority, glory, and sovereign dominion. He is one from among men to whom is given divine prerogatives. Since only God can receive such prerogatives, the Son of man is a God-man (Dan. 10:16). Thus, the Son of Man, Jesus, descended from heaven (John 3:13) and was dependent on God, as He had nowhere to lay His head (Matt. 8:20). He exercises an authoritative and redemptive mission (John 3:14). He is the universal Lord (Matt. 28:18; cf. Dan. 7:13-14) and has total responsibility and authority for judging the world (Matt. 13:41-42; 19:28).

NASB, NIV, NKJV, RSV: Son of Man
LB: the Messiah (note: Lit., "the Son of Man")

G. Vos, *The Self-Disclosure of Jesus* (Grand Rapids: Eerdmans, 1954).

118
sons of the prophets (1 Kings 20:35)
HEBREW: *mibbᵉnê hannᵉbîʾîm*

Key passages for the significance of this phrase are 1 Kings 20:35 and Amos 7:14. The Hebrew phrase consists of the noun *bᵉnê*, the plural construct of *bēn* ("son") and the plural noun *nᵉbîʾîm* ("prophets"). The same form occurs in 2 Kings 2:7; 5:22; and 9:1. The form with the prefixed preposition omitted appears in 2 Kings 2:3, 5, 15; 4:1, 38; 6:1; and 9:7—where "son" is used in the sense of a disciple or follower, rather than in a literal, physical sense.

The "sons" were prophets who stood in a close and intimate relationship to the master prophets Elijah and Elisha. There were groups of such sons at least in Bethel and Jericho (2 Kings 2). They may have been married (2 Kings 4:1) and may have lived in their own separate communities (2 Kings 6:1). It is interesting that Amos makes a point of stating that he was neither a prophet nor of prophetic descent (Amos 7:14).

NASB, NIV, NKJV, RSV: sons of the prophets
LB: one of the prophets

E. J. Young, *My Servants the Prophets* (Grand Rapids: Eerdmans, 1952), pp. 66, 93.

119
the spirits in prison (1 Pet. 3:19)
GREEK: *tois en phulakēi pneumasin*

This phrase consists of the definite article *tois* and the noun it modifies, *pneumasin*, and encloses the modifying prepositional phrase—the preposition *en* ("in") and its object *phulakēi* ("prison"). Some scholars argue that "spirits" does not refer to angels or to men living on the earth but to the souls of men already dead (cf. Heb. 12:23; Rev. 6:9; 20:4). The context tells us that these are the spirits of those who rejected Noah's preaching. After the resurrection, Christ in His spirit descended into that part of hades where the spirits of Noah's contemporaries were imprisoned and preached to them. He did this not that they might believe, but that in hearing the gospel they would continue in their unbelief and vindicate divine justice. However, the clear teaching of other Scripture passages is that after death there is no witness to the ungodly and no benefit of earthly intercession on their behalf. On the other hand, many scholars argue that the spirits of Noah's contemporaries were prisoners (their condition) in prison (their location) in Peter's day, and that in Noah's day Jesus had preached to them in His spirit through Noah. A particularly concise statement is found in *The Criswell Study Bible:*

This passage is one of the most difficult to interpret in the Bible, there being more than ninety variations of interpretations attempted by Christian scholars since the second century. Generally, however, these may be reduced to four plausible understandings: (1) Jesus descended into *hades* (the realm of the dead) between His crucifixion and resurrection to proclaim judgment upon those condemned in the O.T. period. (2) Jesus descended into *tartarus*, the place of confinement for fallen angels, to proclaim judgment to them. (3) Jesus descended into a realm of hades known as *paradise*, in which O.T. saints were held until the atonement could be actually accomplished. The preaching would be the message of the finished atonement at Golgotha. (4) The Spirit of Christ (cf. 1 Pet. 1:11) preached through Noah concerning impending judgment to the disobedient spirits of men in the antediluvian (pre-flood) civilization. The latter two views are the more popular among evangelicals and are also the most feasible. The third view offers explanation of Ephesians 4:8-9 to the effect that Christ descended to the lower parts of the earth and led captivity captive (a reference to the loosing of Old Testament saints). The fourth view better explains the specific mention of the antediluvians and their disobedience. It is in accord with Peter's assessment of Noah as "a preacher of righteousness" (cf. 2 Pet. 2:5). In this fourth view, also, fewer difficulties are involved in harmonizing the statements of Jesus from the cross "Today shalt thou be with me in paradise" (Luke 23:43) and "Father, into thy hands I commend my spirit" (Luke 23:46). (1454-55)

NASB: the spirits now in prison
RSV, LB, NIV, NKJV: the spirits in prison

W. A. Criswell, ed., *The Criswell Study Bible* (Nashville: Nelson, 1979).

120
strain at a gnat (Matt. 23:24)
   GREEK: *diulizontes ton kōnōpa*

This phrase occurs only in Jesus' denunciation of the Pharisees: "Ye blind guides, which strain at a gnat, and swallow a camel." Although the meaning of the sentence is obvious enough and offers no difficulties, a closer look will show the common translation to be in error. The rare verbal form *diulizontes* (actually a participle) means "to strain out," particularly to filter something out of a drink. In his *Historia Animalium* Aristotle describes a tiny worm found to infest wine and called konopa, undoubtedly a species of nematode, often called "vinegar eel." The Greeks probably used the term for such worms and for the water-borne larvae of mosquitoes. It is the Greek word used in Matt. 23:24.

The word, however, was also used for "mosquito," and the Latin Vulgate translates it as *culicem* ("mosquito" or "fly"). The Lindesfarne Gospels (950) read *Latuas blindo gie worthias thone fleze* ("blind leaders who strain out a fly"). Apparently "gnat" in early British English was used for any small flying insect of the order Diptera, including true gnats, mosquitoes, and flies. Thus the translation of Wycliffe (1380) introduced the reading "blinde leders clensenge a gnat," which Tyndale (1534) followed, "Ye blinde gydes which strayne out a gnat."

Here we discover another peculiar shift. From 1534 the English versions use the preposition "out," but the Rheims version (1582) introduced a twist in the phrase and reads "that straine a gnat," omitting the "out." The KJV (1611) thus misreads the text and translates "which strain *at a* gnat." The best reading of the phrase appears to be "You blind guides who strain out a mosquito and swallow a camel." This text has the singular importance of demonstrating Jesus' sense of humor, a most interesting and little discussed aspect of the incarnation.

NASB, NIV, NKJV, LB: strain out a gnat
RSV: straining out a gnat

121
as **strangers and pilgrims** (1 Pet. 2:11)
GREEK: *hōs paroikous kai parepidēmous*

This phrase, which occurs only in 1 Pet. 2:11, is a dependent clause introduced by the comparative particle *hōs* ("as," "like," "in such a way"), with the noun *paroikous*, the simple conjunction *kai* ("and"), and the noun *parepidēmous*. These same two nouns are used in the Septuagint to describe Abraham's relationship to the land as he bargained to buy a family burial place (Gen. 23:4). The Greek *paroikos* (Hebrew *gēr*) was one who dwelt in a land or town but had no citizenship or civil rights there. He was not a citizen, but a permanent dweller with considerable freedom. In the New Testament words built on the verb *paroikeō* are used of Israel's stay in Egypt (Acts 13:17), of Moses' stay in Midian (Acts 7:29), and of Abram's and his family's stay on earth (Heb. 11:13), reflecting the Gen. 23:4 passage.

The *parepidēmos* had fewer rights than the *paroikos*, but was a temporary, landless wage earner. This word speaks of the lack of a true home. The epistle of 1 Peter is addressed to the pilgrims (*parepidēmoi*) of the Christian dispersion. In describing Christians as sojourners and pilgrims, Peter emphasizes that our true citizenship and home are in heaven.

NASB, NIV: as aliens and strangers
NKJV: as sojourners and pilgrims
RSV: as aliens and exiles
LB: you are only visitors here

122
for a sweetsmelling savour (Eph. 5:2)
GREEK: *eis osmēn euōdias*

This phrase occurs in Eph. 5:2 (cf. Phil. 4:18) but is based on Hebrew Old Testament usage. It is a prepositional phrase introduced by the preposition *eis* (here indicating the goal toward which the main action of the sentence is directed), then the noun *osmēn* ("aroma"), which is modified by the adjective *euōdias* ("good," "sweet").

The phrase "sweet-smelling fragrance" is well known from the Old Testament Mosaic period as a description of nonexpiatory sacrifices (almost exclusively). It first occurs in connection with the sacrifice Noah offered when leaving the ark (Gen 8:21), but also occurs frequently of various Old Testament Mosaic sacrifices (as in Lev. 1:9, 13, 17; etc,). In all, the phrase occurs 43 times in the Old Testament. That the Hebrew *rêaḥ* means "odor" or "that which is smelled" is contested by almost no one, but the meaning of *nîḥōaḥ*, however, has elicited some discussion. It appears to be related to the verb *nûaḥ*, signifying "to rest," "to settle down." If this is so, *nîḥōaḥ* might be understood as "placating" (or soothing), "that which settles down divine wrath" and therefore pleases Him. This is supported by the use of the equivalent New Testament phrase in Phil. 4:18, where Paul describes the Philippians' gift to him as a "sweet smell (*osmēn euōdias*), a sacrifice acceptable, well pleasing to God." In Eph. 5:2 Christ's offering and sacrifice carries the connotation of a placating odor (cf. Gen. 8:21), rather than the later Old Testament restriction of this phrase essentially to nonexpiatory sacrifice. Under Moses there was no way man could placate God with His sacrifice.

NASB: fragrant aroma
NIV, RSV: fragrant offering
NKJV: sweet-smelling aroma
LB: sweet perfume

T

123

tabering upon their breasts (Nah. 2:7 [H v. 8])
HEBREW: $m^e\dot{t}\bar{o}pp\bar{o}t$ 'al-$libb\bar{e}hen$

    This Hebrew phrase occurs only in Nah. 2:7. Grammatically it consists of a participle modified by a prepositional phrase. The intensive mood of the participle suggests continual action. In form this noun is rare in two respects. First, the usual plural of $l\bar{e}b$ is $libbot$, and second, the $yodh$ usually appears when a plural is written. The noun most often means "heart," although, as here, it can sometimes represent the area over the heart, that is, the breast. The Hebrew verb $t\bar{a}pap$ denotes the action of beating or playing a tambourine or timbrel, as in Ps. 68:25. In Nahum this word, which ordinarily pictures a joyous act, is used to express deepest agony and mourning. Similarly, in the New Testament the publican beat on his breast in remorse (Luke 18:13).

NASB: Beating on their breasts (note: Lit., "hearts")
NIV: beat upon their breasts
NKJV, RSV: Beating their breasts
LB: beat their breasts

124

the tabernacle of your Moloch and Chiun your images (Amos 5:26)
HEBREW: '$\bar{e}t$ $sikk\hat{u}t$ $malk^ekem$ $w^e\bar{e}t$ $k\hat{i}y\hat{u}n$ $\dot{s}alm\hat{e}kem$

    This phrase occurs only in Amos 5:26 and consists of two parallel units, each introduced by the sign of the direct object ('$\bar{e}t$). Each subunit consists of two nouns in apposition, with the first noun being a proper name and the second a description. The kem is the second person plural pronoun. The proper names are held to be names of Near Eastern deities, repointed with the vowels of the Hebrew word $shiqq\hat{u}\dot{s}$ ("abomination"). The Masoretic accentuation fits the structural contours of the verse, creating a problem in the case of $\dot{s}alm\hat{e}kem$. $Malk^em$ is a singular noun with a plural pronoun appended ("your king"). $\dot{S}alm\hat{e}kem$ is a plural noun with suffix. Structurally, these two nouns are parallel. The sec-

ond, however, modifies a singular noun, the proper name *Chiun*. Literally, the second unit reads "and Chiun your images"—a difficult phrase as
the translations attest.

Both of these appellations are described in the text as "the star of
your god." "Star" is the Assyrian word (*Kaawann*) for the planet Saturn,
known in Hebrew as *kaivan*. According to Amos, Israel's political sub-
mission to Assyria involved worshiping Assyrian gods, which most certainly would result in divine judgment.

NASB: You also carried along Sikkuth your king and Kiyyun, your images
NIV: the shrine of your king, the pedestal of your idols (note: Or, "Sak-
     kuth your king/ and Kaiwan your idols")
NKJV: You also carried Sikkuth your king / And Chiun, your idols
RSV: You shall take up Sakkuth your king, and Kaiwan, your star-god
LB: in Sakkuth your king, and in Kaiwan, your god of the stars

125

that no prophecy of the scripture is of any private interpretation (2 Pet.
1:20)
   GREEK: *hoti pasa prophēteia graphēs idias epiluseōs ou ginetai*

This phrase occurs only in 2 Pet. 1:20, in a declaration of the authority and authenticity of the apostolic message. The phrase is not basically
Greek but Hebraic in construction. The idea really begins back at verse
19: "And we have the word of the prophets made more certain, and you
will do well to pay attention to it, as to a light shining in a dark place,
until the day dawns and the morning star rises in your hearts. Above
all, you must understand . . ." (NIV). That long explanation points
toward the conclusion of which the phrase is a part.

The first word, *hoti*, is a common conjunction often used with verbs
of knowing, understanding, and the like. Next comes the common
adjective *pasa* ("all"), modifying the following noun, *prophēteia* ("prophecy"). *Graphēs*, usually translated "Scripture," refers to the Old Testament, especially so because the verb in the next sentence (v. 21) is in
the past tense called the aorist (see Introduction).

The next two words are the source of some of the difficulties with the
text: *idias*, the common adjective denoting possession ("one's own"), followed by the noun *epiluseōs*, which is used only here in the New Testament. It is in the genitive case with the verb *ginetai*, in a construction
called the genitive of the possessor—the possessor in this case being
indicated by the adjective. The idea is that the prophecy is not set forth
by a human being who necessarily understands what he is writing, but
comes from *over and above* the prophet's own understanding. The text

should thus read "that no prophecy of Scripture is a matter of the one's personal interpretation." The one distinctly referred to here is the prophet through whom the God-breathed message comes. The issue is not whether individuals within the church are permitted to interpret Scripture. To make that clear several contemporary versions supply the word *prophet* for the adjective *one's*. Such a reading of the text fits in very well with another Petrine passage (1 Pet. 1:10-12).

The Criswell Study Bible states in a note on this passage, "The terminology in Greek says that no prophecy came into being through anyone's personal disclosure" (p. 1459). The confusion over the text in the English tradition goes back to Wycliffe (1380), who translated, "And first under stonde ye this thing that eche profecie of scripture: is not made bi propre interpretacioun." The reading "propre" (which gives no clue that it stands for "prophet") is found in a direct borrowing from the Vulgate, which reads, *propria interpretatione non fit* ("not of one's own interpretation").

NASB: no prophecy of Scripture is a matter of one's own interpretation
NIV: no prophecy of Scripture came about by the prophet's own interpretation
NKJV: no prophecy of Scripture is of any private interpretation
RSV: no prophecy of scripture is a matter of one's own interpretation
LB: no prophecy recorded in Scripture was ever thought up by the prophet himself

126
they shoot out the lip (Ps. 22:7 [H v. 8])
HEBREW: *yapṭîrû bᵉśāpāh*

This phrase occurs only in Ps. 22:7 and consists of the verb *pāṭar* in the causative stem, followed by the prepositional phrase, which is comprised of the preposition *bᵉ*, prefixed to the singular *śāpāh*. This verb is rather rare in biblical literature, occurring but eight times, and only once in this stem. In three passages it has to do with escaping—"getting out" or "letting out" (1 Sam. 19:10; 2 Chron. 23:8; Prov. 17:14). In the rest of its occurrences (the fourth usage) in the base stem, it has to do with being open, as with flowers (see 1 Kings 6:18). In the first three uses one can discern a parallel to Akkadian *paṭāru*. Our phrase appears to be related to the fourth usage and, therefore, refers to an opening of the mouth—literally, "they cause to open with the mouth" in insulting gestures and speech. Because this is a rare use of the verb, the phrase is decidedly difficult to render precisely.

NASB: They separate with the lip
NIV: they hurl insults
NKJV: They shoot out the lip
RSV: they make mouths at me
LB: and sneers

127
These are the generations (Gen. 2:4)
HEBREW: *'ēlleh tôlᵉdôt*

This phrase is found eleven times in Genesis (2:4; 5:1; 6:9; 10:1; 11:10, 27; 25:12, 19; 36:1, 9; 37:2). These are the actual introductions to the sections of the book, which is in ten separate but related histories. The phrase appears in a few other Old Testament genealogical contexts—in effect, picking up from the Genesis use of the phrase. The whole of Genesis can be outlined on this basis. The phrase is used in each case as the summary-introduction to the section which follows. The book may be organized as follows:

1. The creation (1:1—2:3)
2. The generations of the heavens and the earth (2:4—4:26)
3. The generations of Adam (5:1—6:8)
4. The generations of Noah (6:9—9:29)
5. The generations of the sons of Noah (10:1—11:9)
6. The generations of Shem (11:10-26)
7. The generations of Terah (11:27—25:11)
8. The generations of Ishmael (25:12-18)
9. The generations of Isaac (25:19—35:29)
10. The generations of Esau (36:1—37:1)
11. The generations of Jacob (37:2—50:26)

NASB, NIV: This is the account
NKJV: This is the history
RSV: These are the generations
LB: Here is a summary

W. White, Jr. "Contemporary Understanding of Genesis 1:1-2:3," in J.H. Skilton, ed., *The Law and the Prophets* (Nutley, N.J.: Presbyterian and Reformed, 1974), pp. 158-73.

128
Thou art my Son (Ps. 2:7)
   HEBREW: *bᵉnî attāh*

This phrase is found only in Ps. 2:7 and consists of the noun *ben* with
an affixed first person pronoun, followed by the second person personal
pronoun. It reads literally "my son, thou art." The verb is understood,
inasmuch as the phrase stands as a complete unit in the text. This
phrase is part of the divine decree relating to David's son and heir. It is
to be taken in connection with 2 Sam. 7:14, "I will be a father to him
and he will be a son to me"—as is made clear in Heb. 1:5.

This is an adoption formula by which God established a special relationship to the king. Obviously, in its Old Testament context it does not
have to do with continuity of essence or being between the Creator and
the creature, man. The New Testament applies the phrase to Christ's
resurrection as the consummation of His exaltation (Acts 13:33; Rom.
1:4; Heb. 1:5). It is also applied at His baptism as the time of His anoint-
ing as messianic king and initiation into His official role as Messiah
(Matt. 3:17; see also Heb. 5:5). Clearly Heb. 5:5 relates the verse to the
taking, or initiation, of His office and to the entirety of Ps. 2:7 (unlike
Matt. 3:17 and parallels). By including "today" the Hebrews passage
emphasizes a time when this sonship was conferred on Christ. The
phrase is also applied to Christ at the transfiguration. Here, in the context of the unveiling of Christ's divine glory, the adoptive royal messianic sonship blends into the ontological sonship (cf. 2 Pet. 1:17).

   NASB: Thou art My Son
   NIV, NKJV, RSV, LB: You are My (my) Son (son)

129
thou knowest that I love thee (John 21:15)
   GREEK: *su oidas hoti philō se*

Occurring only in John 21:15, this phrase consists of the personal pronoun *su*, the verb *oidas* (aorist, a special past tense), the particle *hoti*,
which introduces a dependent clause representing what is known, and
the verb *phileō* and its direct object *se* ("you"). In the famous exchange
between Jesus and Peter after the resurrection, Jesus began by asking
Peter if he loved Him (*agapē* love) with the intelligent, purposeful,
whole-hearted love arising out of the entire personality—and if he did
so more than the other disciples. Peter, shaken by his relapse, deigned
neither to compare his feelings with others nor to aver such strong,

deep commitment. He simply replied that he loved Jesus with a love arising primarily out of emotion (*philia* love), a love that may not be so strong and mature. Indeed, he said that Jesus knew (*oida*) this to be a fact. Jesus asked him to examine himself again, this time not in comparison with others, but to see if there was any *agapē* love in him. Peter made the same response. Finally, Jesus asked Peter if he loved Him with *philia* love. Peter then replied that Jesus, who knows (*oida*) all things discerns (*ginōskō*) that he does love Him with *philia* love.

NASB, NIV, NKJV, RSV: You know (that) I love You
LB: You know I am your friend

130
Thou sayest (Matt. 27:11)
GREEK: *su legeis*

A significant and primary appearance of this phrase is in Matt. 27:11 (see also Matt. 26:25, 64). It consists of the second person personal pronoun and the present active indicative, second person singular verb, and is a strong assertion of a truth previously questioned. Matthew's account is expanded and explained by John, who gives Jesus' fuller response: "Thou sayest that I am a king. To this end was I born, and for this cause came I into the world, that I should bear witness unto the truth. Every one that is of the truth heareth my voice" (John 18:37). In other words, "Thou sayest" is elliptical, probably colloquial, for "Indeed you say what is true." When Judas asked, "Am I the betrayer," Jesus responded, "[Indeed], you say [the truth]" (Matt. 26:25). The phrase is a strong assertion of a fact.

NASB, NKJV: It is as you say
NIV: Yes, it is as you say
RSV: You have said so
LB: "Yes," Jesus replied

131
Thou shalt not kill (Ex. 20:13)
HEBREW: *lōʾ tirṣāḥ*

This simple and straightforward phrase appears in the Ten Commandments in both Ex. 20:13 and Deut. 5:17. It consists of the negative adverb *lōʾ* followed by the base or Qal stem of the verb *rāṣaḥ* in the second person form. Problems concerning the meaning of the phrase center on the exact meaning of the verbal root. It appears 38 times in the Old Testament, referring exclusively to the violent death of a human being. In all but one instance it refers to the killing of one human being by another. In the one exception (Prov. 22:13), it refers to the killing of a human being by an animal. Since it is the enormity of the act that is the primary focus of the term, many have proposed that *rāṣaḥ* has in view the intentional act of killing, that is, murder. However, the verb appears 14 times in relation to the cities of refuge, to which those accused of the *accidental* killing of another human being were instructed to flee. Thus modern versions often avoid the translation "murder" in those passages and indicate a difference between murder and manslaughter that is not necessarily intrinsic in the verb. The range of meanings includes "murder," "slay," "kill (a human being)".

In the Ten Commandments it seems that the basic principle of the violent killing of another human being, regardless of the motive or means, is involved. Whatever other degrees of killing they may encompass, however, the passages in Ex. 20 and Deut. 5 are absolute prohibitions against murder. There have been occasional interpretations of the phrase to include the killing of any warm-blooded creature—even the slaughter of animals for food. But such a notion is clearly not covered by the verb *rāṣaḥ*.

The command is repeated in the New Testament in five passages. In Matt. 5:21 it is quoted verbatim from the Septuagint (Greek) renderings of the Exodus and Deuteronomy passages (*ou phoneuseis*, a phrase consisting of the negative particle followed by the finite verb in the future tense). The Latin Vulgate follows the same construction, reading *Non occides*. The commandment appears again in a less direct style in the conversation of Jesus with the rich young ruler (Mark 10:19; Luke 18:20). In both of these passages the phrase appears in the subjunctive construction (*mē phoneusēis*), although the meaning is essentially the same. The negative particle is the form used with the subjunctive of the verb. This less vivid rendering is also used in James 2:11, in its only appearance outside of the gospels. In Romans 13:9 the stronger direct quote from the Septuagint Greek of Exodus is used, precisely like the Matthew citation in the Sermon on the Mount.

NASB, NIV, NKJV: You shall not murder
RSV: You shall not kill
LB: You must not murder

132

the **tree of life** (Gen. 2:9; Rev. 2:7)

    HEBREW: *'ēş haḥayyîm*

    GREEK: *xulou tēs zōēs*

This phrase is remarkably difficult to explain. It first occurs in Gen. 2:9; 3:22, 24—all in the narrative of the Garden of Eden. It consists of the common Semitic word *'ēş* (*tree*) in a construct relationship with *ḥayyîm*, an abstract noun meaning "endless life" or "life at its highest." Three things are clear about the use of the phrase here: (1) the fact that *'ēş* has the definite article attached demonstrates that this was a particular tree already known to the readers; (2) the tree of life was planted in the sacred garden, the paradise that was the habitation of God; and it was man's nearness to God in the garden that imparted life, and the symbol of this communion was the tree; and (3) the tree of life has eschatological significance, as seen in the reference to it in Ezek. 31:3-9; 47:12; and Rev. 2:7; 22:2, 14, 19. G. Vos makes the interpretation of the tree very clear:

> It appears from Gen. 3:22 that man previous to his probation had not eaten it, while yet nothing is recorded concerning any prohibition which seems to point to the understanding that the use of the tree was reserved for the future, quite in agreement with the eschatological significance attributed to it later. The tree was associated with the higher, the unchangeable, the eternal life to be secured through the probation. Anticipation of the result by a present enjoyment of the fruit would have been out of keeping with its sacramental character. After man should have been made sure of the attainment of the highest life, the tree would appropriately have been the sacramental means for communicating the highest life. After the fall God attributes to man the inclination of snatching the fruit against the divine purpose. But this very desire implies the understanding that it somehow was the specific life-sacrament for the time after the probation. According to Rev. 2:7 it is to him "that overcometh" that God promises to give of the tree of life in the midst of his paradise. The effort to obtain the fruit after the fall would have meant a desperate attempt to steal the fruit where the title to it had been lost, Gen. 3:22. (*Biblical Theology* [Grand Rapids: Eerdmans, 1954], 38-39).

The phrase "the tree of life" is also used in Proverbs in four passages (3:18; 11:30; 13:12; 15:4). Although these uses show no relation to those in Genesis, they do indicate that, by the later years of the Old Testament (assuming a late date for Proverbs), the phrase was commonplace in the typical folk wisdom of the time, and thus came into the royal wisdom. The book of Revelation repeats many themes from the account of the origin of history in Genesis. The citation in Revelation is exactly the same phrase (*xulou tēs zōēs*) as the Septuagint version of the Genesis passages.

The versions cited all read "Tree of Life" or "tree of life."

133
the **tree of the knowledge of good and evil** (Gen. 2:9)
HEBREW: *'ēṣ hada'at ṭôb wārā'*

This phrase occurs only twice in the Bible (Gen. 2:9, 17). The same tree seems to be referred to in Gen. 3:3 as "the tree which is in the midst of the garden," from which Adam and Eve ate the forbidden fruit. This experiential knowledge of "good and evil" is directly related to their partaking of the fruit of that tree (3:5, 22).

The overall phrase is best understood by searching out the meaning of "good and evil." As G. Vos points out,

> If now we enquire how maturity designated as 'knowledge of good and evil' was to be attained, either in a desirable or in an undesirable sense, regard must be first of all had to the exact form of the phrase in Hebrew. The phrase is not 'knowledge of good and the evil.' It reads literally translated: 'knowledge of good-and-evil,' i.e., of good and evil as correlated, mutually conditioned concepts. Man was to attain something he had not before. He was to learn the good in its clear opposition to the evil." (*Biblical Theology*, pp. 41-42)

"Good and evil" is connected to the plural ("gods") in Gen. 3:5 and to "us" in 3:22. As Cassuto has written, "In the first of these verses it is possible and in the second it is certain, that the reference is to the angels of God. Elsewhere it is stated specifically in relation to an angel (2 Sam. 14:17)" (*A Commentary on the Book of Genesis*, pt. 1 [Jerusalem: Hebrew U. Press, 1961], p. 113). The idea is that Adam and Eve were without any knowledge of moral conflict. But once having become "wise" about the moral dilemma of the world, their disobedience of God's command caused them to fall. The results of that fall into sin and God's dealing with it are the great dual theme of the rest of Scripture.

NASB, NIV, NKJV, RSV: the tree of the knowledge of good and evil
LB: Tree of Conscience

134

through philosophy and vain deceit (Col. 2:8)

GREEK: *dia tēs philosophias kai kenēs apatēs*

This phrase occurs only in Col. 2:8 and has been the subject of much study over the centuries. It is a straightforward prepositional phrase with *dia* ("through") governing two nouns, one with the definite article *tēs* and the other modified by an adjective. The first noun, *philosophias*, always transliterated in English as "philosophy," is of course related to the noun *philosophos* ("philosopher"; used only in Acts 17:18). In both passages the terms have decidedly negative connotations. The second noun of the phrase is *apatēs* ("deception" or "deceitfulness," as in Matt. 13:22; Mark 4:19; Eph. 4:22; 2 Thess. 2:10; Heb. 3:13). This noun is modified by the adjective *kenēs* ("empty," as in Mark 12:3; Luke 1:53; Eph. 5:6). The absence of the article with the second noun in effect means the two are used synonymously.

"Philosophy" in this phrase does not refer exclusively to Greek sophistry and wisdom. Josephus refers to the teachings of the Essenes, Sadducees, and Pharisees as "philosophy" (*Antiquities* 18:2, 1). In fact, as a further comment on the phrase, Paul says, "After the tradition of men, after the rudiments of the world." The term "rudiments" (*stoicheia*) refers to the systems of organization of natural phenomena found in the Hellenistic cults. These involved the signs of the zodiac and the hierarchies of beings in Gnosticism. The combination of late Jewish cultic teachings and oriental mysticism produced the "philosophies" that plagued Christianity during its first three centuries. In light of these meanings it appears that the best translation of Col. 2:8 is, "Take care lest there shall be anyone who leads you away as captive through philosophy and empty deception according to the schemes of the world."

NASB: through philosophy and empty deception
NIV: through hollow and deceptive philosophy
NKJV: through philosophy and empty deceit
RSV: by philosophy and empty deceit
LB: with their philosophies, their wrong and shallow answers

U

135
Understandest thou what thou readest? (Acts 8:30)
   GREEK: *ara ge ginōskeis ha anaginōskeis*

This phrase constitutes the question Philip asked the Ethiopian eunuch as he read from Isa. 52:13—53:12, a Servant of the Lord song. It consists of the particle *ara* strengthened by the particle *ge* and the present active indicative verb *ginōskeis* and its objective clause, with its relative pronoun and present active indicative verb *anaginōskeis*. *Ara*, used where a response is expected denying what was asked, shows that Philip politely suggested that the eunuch did not really understand what he was reading. Philip was suggesting that he knew what the eunuch was reading, that he knew the deeper and true meaning of the passage, how it had been fulfilled in Christ, and that he was willing to explain it to the eunuch. The verb *ginōskeis* primarily means "to know," but to know in the sense of understanding, rather than of merely being aware, as does *oida*. In the present tense, *ginōskeis* was used to ask not if the eunuch would eventually understand, but if he then understood, what he was reading. The plural pronoun *ha* ("what" or "what things") shows that Philip was asking a question in particular rather than in general— not "Do you understand the Bible passage in general?" but "Do you understand the various particulars of the passage?" The verb *anaginōskeis* in the present tense was used to ask if the eunuch understood these things as he was presently reading. The eunuch's reading and Philip's inquiry are viewed as a unit. The force of the grammar focuses specifically on the eunuch's understanding of the full, messianic meaning and significance of what he was reading.

NASB, NIV, NKJV, RSV: Do you understand what you are reading?
LB: Do you understand it?

136
until Shiloh come (Gen. 49:10)
   HEBREW: *'ad kî-yābō' shîlōh*

This phrase appears only in Gen. 49:10 and consists of the preposition 'ad plus the particle kî, which together form the introduction to a temporal clause. The clause does not speak of replacing what has just been mentioned—as though when Shiloh comes Judah's dominion would cease. Rather it speaks of fulfilling. That is, when Shiloh comes, Judah's dominion would be perfected. The verb yābōʾ (third person singular imperfect) is followed by its object, the noun shîlōh, which may be related to the root shālāh ("be at rest"). Some see in shîlōh a reference to the town Shiloh, but Judah's dominion over the nations was not realized at the assembling of all Israel at Shiloh or with the concomitant events (Josh. 13:1). Nor was this preceded by Judah's dominion over Israel, as prophesied in Gen. 49:8-9.

Others see in the phrase an appellative noun shîlōh and render it "till rest comes" or "till he comes to a place of rest"—but such is grammatically impossible. It is best to see here a messianic prophecy, first fulfilled in Solomon, David's son. Like the word *Shiloh*, the name *Solomon* is built on a root meaning "peace and rest." But Solomon's peace and rest was temporary and limited to Israel. Solomon prophetically spoke of a greater man of peace than himself, a scion of David whose dominion would be worldwide (Ps. 72). After Solomon, the prophets pointed to a Prince of Peace, David's true Son, who would rule the world in peace and righteousness, and whom the world would seek (Isa. 9:5-6; 11:1-10). Ezekiel prophesied the overthrow of the Davidic kingdom until He should come to whom it rightfully belongs (21:27). In this "until he come whose right it is," Ezekiel takes up the Shiloh prophecy, which he expands by relating it to Ps. 72:1-5. The peace and rest of the eternal Davidic kingdom would find its fulfillment in the Prince of Peace, Jesus Christ. He is the true Shiloh, the true King of righteousness and peace, the final Son of Judah (Heb. 7:2, 11, 14, 17), the Lion of Judah (Rev. 5:5), and our peace (Eph. 2:14) and final rest (Heb. 4).

NASB, NKJV: Until Shiloh comes
NIV: until he comes to whom it belongs (note: Or, "until Shiloh comes";
    or, "until he comes to whom tribute belongs")
RSV: until he comes to whom it belongs
LB: until Shiloh comes (note: "he to whom it belongs")

137
Ur of the Chaldees (Gen. 11:28)
HEBREW: 'ûr kaśdîm

This phrase occurs four times in the Old Testament, always in the context of Abraham's migration from his ancestral homeland to Canaan

(Gen. 11:28, 31; Neh. 9:7). The phrase appears to consist of a Sumerian place-name and a gloss (a phrase or term added to explain it). The Sumerian name is *Uri(m)*, the proper noun "Ur" being an ancient city in lower Mesopotamia, but also the general term for "city." There may, in fact, be another site in view as Abraham's home, since the Ebla tablets seem to mention a town by this name in northern Mesopotamia. The other word, the gloss, is *kaśdîm*, from a possible confusion of two Mesopotamian peoples—the Kassites (Akkadian *kashshu[m]*) and the much later Kaldeans, or Chaldeans (from Akkadian *kaldu[m]*), who overran the area of ancient Sumer about 1000 B.C. They became the rulers of ancient Babylonia when King Ashurbanipal of Assyria set the Chaldean noble Kandalanu on the throne of Babylon (648 B.C.). A few years later (Sept. 23, 626 B.C.), another Chaldean, Nabopolassar, became king and founded the eleventh dynasty, the Chaldean or Neo-Babylonian. It is from this dynasty, well over a thousand years after Abraham, that the prepositional phrase "of the Chaldeans" may be traced. The gloss was probably supplied to identify the original Ur, whether it was in upper or lower Mesopotamia, after it had faded from memory. The shift in spelling from "k" to "ch" came by way of the Greek, which transliterated the Akkadian/ Babylonian *kaldu(m)* as *chaldaioi*, which was in turn read as *Chaldeorum* (genitive plural) by the Latin Vulgate, through which the form came into English.

All versions cited read "Ur of the Chaldeans."

138
uttermost parts of the sea (Ps. 139:9)
HEBREW: *bᵉaḥarît yām*

Appearing only in Ps. 139:9, this prepositional phrase opens with the prefixed preposition *bᵉ* followed by its object, the feminine construct noun *'aḥarît*, and the noun *yām* ("sea"). *'Aḥarît* is a superlative noun, formed from *'aḥar* ("after," "behind-of place," "afterwards") and here carries the idea of westernmost. The word *yām* is the usual Hebrew word for sea, but here it may mean "west." The phrase therefore means "farthest limits of the western sea," "farthest west," or "most distant west"—as borne out by the structure of vv. 8-9. The overall thrust of these verses is that there is no place the psalmist could go to escape God's presence—whether to heaven or hell (Sheol), to the farthest east (the wings of the morning, where the sun rises), or to the farthest west.

NASB: the remotest part of the sea
NIV: on the far side of the sea
NKJV, RSV: the uttermost parts of the sea
LB: to the farthest oceans

V

139
valley of the shadow of death (Ps. 23:4)
  HEBREW: *bᵉgêʾ ṣalmāwet*

Occurring only in Ps. 23:4, this phrase consists of the preposition *bᵉ* prefixed to the singular construct noun *gêʾ*, followed by the noun *ṣalmāwet*, on which much discussion has centered. Philologically the term has been related to Akkadian *ṣalamu* ("be dark") plus an *-ut* abstract ending. On the basis of the Hebrew pointing and the punctuation of many versions (including renderings of the Matt. 4:16 quote from the Septuagint), the traditional explanation has been to see here a compound word: *ṣal* ("shadow") and *māwet* ("death"). There is cause to reconsider this etymology, however, even though it follows traditional philology.

A study of the use of the word in the Old Testament reveals that it is often a synonym of darkness, connoting deepest darkness (e.g., Job 16:16; 28:3). In other passages it represents the "darkness" of death. In Job 38:17 the gates of *ṣalmāwet* are the "gates of death," and in Jer. 2:6 *ṣalmāwet* represents death as an attribute of the desert. Job speaks of going to the land of no return (10:21-22), well known in Akkadian literature as the abode of the dead, the land of darkness and *ṣalmāwet* ("deepest darkness"). Only in Ps. 23:4 and perhaps Ps. 107:10, 14 (if one allows the traditional etymology) does the word refer to a brush with death rather than the very presence of death. It would seem more consistent with its use elsewhere in biblical literature to understand *ṣalmāwet* in these two psalms either as "deepest darkness" or "death's darkness." Since in Ps. 23:4 the allusion is clearly not to death itself, "deepest darkness" (*like* the darkness of death) is the preferred translation.

NASB, RSV: the valley of the shadow of death (note: Or, "the valley of deepest darkness")

NIV: the valley of the shadow of death (note: Or, "through the darkest valley")

NKJV: the valley of the shadow of death

LB: the dark valley of death

140
Verily, verily, I say unto you (John 1:51)
GREEK: *amēn amēn legō humin*

The introduction of many of Jesus' statements with this double asseverative particle is found only in John's gospel (1:51; 3:3, 5, 11; 5:19, 24, 25; 6:26, 32, 47, 53; 8:34, 58; 10:1, 7; 12:24; 13:16, 20, 21, 38; 14:12; 16:20, 23; 21:18). In a number of cases the same idea expressed in the John passage is expressed in one of the epistles, but in only two cases are there clear parallels between John and the other gospels (John 13:16 with Luke 6:40 and John 13:20 with Matt. 10:40). Only John introduces the statements with "verily, verily." The Greek is a direct transliteration of the Hebrew. It is interesting that the Gothic version of Ulfilas (375), while translating all of the other Greek of the New Testament, transliterated the double *amēn*.

There is no doubt that the use of the term before a particularly important statement was a feature of Jesus' speech. It is rather amazing that no English version has ever used the term as it is in the original, following the Greek and the Latin Vulgate. The attempt at translating, rather than transliterating, the double particle is found in English versions as early as the Lindesfarne Gospels (950), in which the term "sothlice" was used. The Old English (1000) introduced "verralye." Wycliffe (1380) used "truli truli I seie to thee," but Tyndale's version of 1534 has "Verely verely," which the KJV and many other later versions followed. The Rheims (1582), being closer to the Latin Vulgate, uses "Amen, Amen."

NASB, RSV: Truly, truly, I say to you
NIV: I tell you the truth
NKJV: Most assuredly, I say to you
LB: With all the earnestness I possess I tell you this

141
a virgin shall conceive (Isa. 7:14)
HEBREW: *hinnēh hā'almāh hārāh*

This clause, occurring only in Isa. 7:14, consists of the particle *hinnēh* ("behold") followed by the subject (the feminine singular noun *'almāh*, with a prefixed definite article) and the verb *hārāh* (feminine singular). *Hinnēh* is used in Ugaritic and Hebrew to introduce statements deserving special attention. The verb *hārāh* usually is used of conception, while *yālad* and *hûl* refer to completion of the birthing process. Hebrew attests three words for woman (*'ishshāh*, *b^etûlāh*, and *'almāh*), the last term representing a young girl of marriageable age who might well be a virgin. English has no single word embracing this range of meaning.

Isa. 7:16 predicts the destruction of "the two kings you dread" before the child would be weaned. When Isaiah's wife bore a son, God pronounced this as the sign that the prophecy concerning the two kings had already begun to be fulfilled. But more than this is envisioned in Isa. 7:14. Isaiah did not use the Hebrew word signifying woman or wife (*'ishshāh*) or *b^etûlāh*, which (like its Ugaritic cognate) means simply a young woman, not necessarily a virgin (see Lev. 21:13, 14; Joel 1:8; etc.). The prophet used *'almāh*, which usually, though also not necessarily (see Gen. 24:43; Song of Sol. 1:3; 6:8), means "virgin." Significantly, the son born to the *'almāh* in Isa. 7 is Immanuel, but Isaiah called his own son Mahar-shalal-hash-baz (8:3). Perhaps by this Isaiah indicated that he did not see in his son the fullness of the prophecy. The New Testament, therefore, quite properly renders *'almāh* by the Greek *parthenos*, meaning "virgin" (Matt. 1:22, 23), as does the the Septuagint for Isa. 7:14. It is noteworthy that the Hebrew reads "the *'almāh* shall conceive"—that is, an *'almāh* as distinct from any other kind of woman. The meaning is best indicated in English by using the indefinite article.

NASB: a virgin will be with child
NIV: The virgin will be with child
NKJV: the virgin shall conceive
RSV: a young woman shall conceive
LB: a child shall be born to a virgin!

E.J. Young, *Studies in Isaiah* (Grand Rapids: Eerdmans, 1954), pp. 143-98.

W

142
without form, and void (Gen. 1:2)
  HEBREW: *tohû wābōhû*

This phrase occurs only twice in the Bible, first in Gen. 1:2, and consists of two nouns joined by the conjunction. Much debate surrounds these two words, and the traditional translation has been defended by many. There is also debate over whether or not the cognates of the two Hebrew words are found in other Semitic languages and literature. Some view the phrase as a description of the state of things following a divine judgment, and posit a gap between Gen. 1:1 and 1:2, during which the creation was inhabited. Exegetically this is thought to be supported primarily by Isa. 45:18, which says, "[God] did not create [the earth] *tohû* but formed [the earth] to be inhabited." But according to Isaiah there were two states of God's creation—the original state in which it was uninhabitable (*tohû*) and the subsequent state, the goal of the creating act, in which the creation was inhabitable. Any rendering that suggests chaos is contrary to the overall thrust of Gen. 1—God's purposeful and all-controlling presence. It would be totally inconsistent with this emphasis to view the first stage of creation as chaotic, confused, and out of control. The phrase rather presents simply a contrast between the uninhabitable creation (cf. Jer. 4:23) and the inhabitable crown of creation, which was a good home for man. This conclusion is buttressed by a consideration of the literary structure of Gen. 1. In the acts of the first three days God gave form to the heavens and earth, and in days four to six He filled them with living creatures, including man.

NASB: formless and void (note: Or, "a waste and emptiness")
NIV: formless and empty
NKjV: without form, and void
RSV: without form and void
LB: a shapeless, chaotic mass (note: Or, "shapeless and void")

E.J. Young, *Studies in Genesis One* (Nutley, N.J.: Presbyterian and Reformed, 1964), pp. 30-38; W. White, Jr., "Contemporary Understanding of Gen. 1:1-2:3," in J.H. Skilton, ed., *The Law and the Prophets* (Nutley, N.J.: Presbyterian and Reformed, 1974), pp. 158-73; R.F. Youngblood, *"tohu"* #2494, in R.L. Harris, G.L. Archer, Jr., B.K. Waltke, eds., *Theological Wordbook of the Old Testament* (Chicago: Moody, 1980), 2:964-65.

143
weeping for Tammuz (Ezek. 8:14)
HEBREW: *mᵉbakkôt et-hattammûz*

This strange phrase, made up of a participle and a proper name, appears only in Ezek 8:14, in the vision of the abominations in Jerusalem. The prophet is told, "Turn thee yet again, and thou shalt see greater abominations that they do. Then he brought me to the door of the gate of the Lord's house which was toward the north; and, behold, there sat women weeping for Tammuz." Tammuz is the Babylonian-Assyrian form of the Sumerian vegetation god Dumuzi. The deity is a prominent figure in a number of Sumerian and Babylonian epics, such as The Adapa Myth and the sixth tablet of the Epic of Gilgamesh, in which it is said to Ishtar, the Babylonian goddess of fertility:

For Tammuz, the lover of your girlhood,
You have commanded weeping year by year.

Tammuz was the vegetation spirit that died with the withering of the grain each year about the end of September. His return to life was celebrated when the new crops appeared in the beginning of the year, which was June-July in the Near East. The fourth month of the year was the season for mourning and became known as "Tammuz," as it is in the present Jewish calendar. The motif of an annually dying and renewing vegetation god is found throughout the ancient world. Tammuz was similar to Adonis of Syria and the Osiris of Egypt and of cults in Canaan, Persia, and among the Hittites. The appalling pagan rites for Tammuz involved sexual and other immoralities commonly connected with fertility cults. But a greater abomination was that of the women of Israel who practiced this primitive and crude cult at the very portal of the Temple (Ezek. 8:14).

The versions cited all read "Tammuz."

144
But **when the Comforter is come** (John 15:26)
GREEK: *Hotan elthēi ho paraklētos*

This phrase appears in John 15:26, but the term *paraklētos* is also used of the Holy Spirit in John 14:16, 26; 16:7 and of Jesus in 1 John 2:1. The phrase consists of the compound *hotan* (a temporal particle which, when used with the aorist subjunctive verb indicates that the action of the dependent clause precedes that of the main clause), the verb *elthēi* (aorist subjunctive), and the definite article *ho*, with the noun *paraklētos* that it modifies. *Paraklētos* ("paraclete" in English transliteration) is passive and literally means "one who is called to another's side." In its various contexts it can mean a legal advocate, an intercessor, a comforter, or a helper in general.

None of these connotations, however, fully captures the breadth and depth of the term when it is used of the Holy Spirit. It is one of the uniquely "Christian" words of New Testament Greek. As Paraclete, the Holy Spirit (1) showed the disciples the things of Christ, (2) taught them things to come, (3) taught them all things, (4) refreshed their memories of Christ's teaching, (5) bears witness to Christ, (6) indwells all believers, (7) performs greater works than Christ did, and (8) convicts of sin, of righteousness, and of judgment. The Paraclete came on the day of Pentecost (Acts 2). In 1 John 2:1 the word is used of Jesus in referring to His work as propitiator of divine wrath.

NASB: When the Helper comes
NIV, RSV: When the Counselor comes
NKJV: But when the Helper comes
LB: But I will send you the Comforter

145
Whose fan is in his hand (Matt. 3:12)
GREEK: *hou to ptuon en tēi cheri autou*

This phrase appears in the sermon of John the Baptist recorded in Matt. 3:12 and Luke 3:17. It consists of the noun *ptoun* ("winnowing fork" or "fan") with the relative pronoun *hou* ("whose"), followed by a straightforward prepositional phrase meaning literally "in-the-hand-his." The interesting word in the phrase is *ptuon*, a Greek technical term that occurs only here in the New Testament, alluding to several passages in the Old. In these passages (Isa. 30:24; Jer. 15:7) the Hebrew word *mizreh*, a participle from the verbal form meaning "to scatter" or "to disperse," carries the specific agricultural meaning of separating grain from its chaff to be carried off by the wind. The Hebrew term occurs only in these two passages and, interestingly enough, the Septuagint translates the first instance with a complex participial form meaning "winnowing," a word related to the verb used in Matt. 21:44 (Luke 20:18). In the second instance the Septuagint translates *diaspora* ("dispersion"), the word used in 1 Pet. 1:1. The picture of God's judgment as a "winnowing" of spiritual wheat and chaff is used in some of the most dramatic and significant passages of Scripture (e.g., Ps. 1:4).

NASB, NIV, NKJV, RSV: His winnowing fork is in His hand
NKJV: His winnowing fan is in His hand
LB: He will separate the chaff from the grain

146
wise men from the east (Matt. 2:1)
   GREEK: *magoi apo anatolōn*

This phrase, appearing only in Matt. 2:1, consists of the masculine plural noun (in the nominative case) modified by the prepositional phrase comprised of *apo* ("from") and its object, *anatolōn* ("east").

The magi ("wise men") are first attested as a tribe of the Median empire somewhere in the seventh century B.C. Their religion was a mixture of ancient beliefs and Zoroastrianism. Basically monotheistic, they worshiped a god who was considered to be the creator of all things and the author of all good. He was opposed by the power of evil in an eternal dualism. The magi had a hereditary priesthood who mediated between their deity and man by means involving blood sacrifice of animals (including horses) and who also practiced divination. They had a concept of unclean animal and vegetable life, which especially included reptiles and insects. They permitted no images in their temples, and the priests dressed in white robes and donned tall, rather conical hats made of felt. The "Rab-mag" of Jer. 39:3, 13 was probably the chief of the magi, the head priest, of his day—"Rab-mag" being a title rather than a name. The magi also figured prominently in the Persian court of Daniel's day as the "magicians" (Dan. 2:10, 27; 4:7, 9; 5:11).

By the time of Christ, magi dominated the Persian-Parthian government, and a special prerogative of their office was the selection of the king. At this time the unpopular Parthian king Phraastes IV was quite old and had already been deposed once before and then been reinstated. Augustus, the Roman emperor was also aged, and Rome lacked an experienced military commander in the region. It was time for the magi to choose a replacement. It is not unlikely that they knew the Jewish Scriptures, especially the writings of Daniel, and Jews had long been citizens, even important governmental servants, in their land. It is of interest that within two years of their appearance before Herod, the magi counsel installed Phraataces as the ruler of Parthia.

NASB: magi from the east
NIV: Magi from the east (note: Traditionally, "Wise Men")
NKJV, RSV: wise men from the East
LB: astrologers from eastern lands

W. White, Jr., "Persia," in M.C. Tenney, ed., *The Zondervan Pictorial Encyclopedia of the Bible* (Grand Rapids: Zondervan, 1975), 4:110-20; D.W. Jayne, "Magi," ibid., 4:31-35.

147
Behold, thou art **wiser than Daniel** (Ezek. 28:3)
HEBREW: *hinnēh ḥākām ʾattāh midānīʾēl*

This phrase occurs in Ezek. 28:3 and consists of the interjection *hinnēh* ("behold"), followed by the noun *ḥākām* ("wise," "skillful") and then the pronoun and the name with the preposition *mîn* (reduced to *m* before the name), meaning "than." The sentence means literally "Behold, you-wiseman-than Daniel," which is translated more meaningfully as "Are you wiser than Daniel?"

But a close look indicates that the name "Daniel" here has a different spelling than in the book of Daniel. The Ezekiel phrase has *dānīʾēl*, whereas in the book of Daniel the name is spelled *dāniyyēʾl* (1:6; et al). There are two other uses of the name in Ezekiel (14:14; 20), both in a list of three: "Noah, Daniel and Job." Since the prophet Daniel lived some one hundred years before Ezekiel, the reference in the book of Ezekiel must be to an earlier Daniel, otherwise unknown in Scripture. The most likely candidate is the sage Danel mentioned in the epics from Ugarit, where the spelling accords well with that in Ezekiel. There is also considerable mention of this Danel in the Tale of Aghat. The father of the hero of this epic is a sage and holy man, Danel, portrayed as continually serving the gods. If this is the Daniel mentioned in Ezekiel, however, a question remains as to why a fictional character from a pagan myth would be mentioned together with Noah and Job. It may be that Danel was a historical character and the author of a famous work of wisdom, so that his name was known both to the authors of the Ugaritic poetry and to the prophet Ezekiel.

NASB, NKJV: Behold, you are wiser than Daniel
NIV: Are you wiser than Daniel? (note: Danel; the Hebrew spelling may suggest a person other than the prophet Daniel.)
RSV: you are indeed wiser than Daniel
LB: You are wiser than Daniel

148

wives, be in subjection (1 Pet. 3:1)
   GREEK: *gunaikes hupotassomenai*

In a day of indulgence and individualism there is perhaps no more troublesome term in all of Scripture than "obedience." The phrase "wives be in subjection" deals specifically with that concept. Although the most important passage for this specific teaching is 1 Pet 3:1, 5, this apostle mentions the general principle of obedience frequently. Using the same Greek verb (*hupotassō*), he exhorts servants (really slaves) to be obedient to their masters (1 Pet. 2:18); younger persons to be obedient to those older (1 Pet. 5:5); believers to be obedient to human government (1 Pet. 2:13); and even all believers to be subject to each other (1 Pet. 5:5). This obedience is to be voluntary, as clearly attested by the use of the verb and its participle throughout Greek literature.

The notion of a wife's obedience to her husband was common throughout the Graeco-Roman world as well as among the Jews. The issue in 1 Peter is not that of some cosmic principle of female subjection to male dominance, but that of winning souls to Christ through exemplary living, and the specific need for believing wives to strive for "a meek and quiet spirit" (1 Pet. 3:4), which is admirable in a man or woman.

NASB, NKJV: be submissive to your own husbands
NIV: be submissive to your husbands
RSV: be submissive
LB: fit in with your husbands' plans

149

wonders in the heavens and in the earth (Joel 2:30 [H 3:3])
   HEBREW: *môpᵉtîm bashshāmayim ûbā'āreṣ*

This phrase, found only in Joel 2:30, is composed of the plural noun *môpᵉtîm* ("wonders") followed by two prepositional phrases, each introduced by the preposition *bᵉ* (with the definite article) and joined by the conjunction. The noun *môpēt* refers to miraculous signs, and first appears in Ex. 4:21, where it refers to the wonders God gave to Moses with which to impress Pharaoh. In the Joel passage the wonders are to appear in the heavens (the usual plural Hebrew word for the heavens, or sky) and the earth (the usual Hebrew word for earth).

This verse and its immediate context are cited by Peter in Acts 2:17-21, where he applies the entire passage to the day of Pentecost. Hence, the "wonders" occurring in the sky may refer to the tongues of fire that descended on the waiting disciples (Acts 2:3). More probably, however, the wonders are those in the eternal heaven, where God dwells and where Jesus was received by the Father, crowned with glory and honor, enthroned at His right hand, and from where Jesus sent forth the Holy Spirit (v. 33-36). The wonders on earth were the resurrection and the miraculous signs (especially the tongues-speaking) displayed at Pentecost. Some scholars refer this part of Peter's citation to the second coming of our Lord, and understand the Greek *terata* ("wonders," Acts 2:19) and its Old Testament precedent (*môp^{e}fîm*) to mean portents, that is, signs that precede and announce the second coming.

NASB: wonders in the sky and on the earth
NIV, NKJV: wonders in the heavens and in (on) the earth
RSV: portents in the heavens and on earth
LB: strange symbols in the earth and sky

150

if any man be a **worshipper of God** (John 9:31)
GREEK: *ean tis theosebēs ēi*

This phrase occurs in the New Testament only in John 9:31, and *theosebēs* ("worshiper") is a hapax legomenon, a word appearing only once (in Scripture). The larger Greek phrase consists of the conjunction *ean* ("if"), the indefinite pronoun *tis* ("anyone"), the noun *theosebēs* (predicate nominative), and the verb *ēi* ("is," present active subjunctive). *Theosebēs* is a compound, consisting of *theo* (from *theos*, meaning "god") and *sebēs* (from *sebō*, meaning "to worship" in the full sense of the word). Used in participial form in the phrase *sebomenou ton theon* (Acts 18:7; cf. 16:14), it refers to a Gentile who attached himself to Judaism by generally practicing Jewish laws, acknowledging the true God as the only God, and frequenting the synagogue—but who did not actually convert to Judaism.

The particular word in our phrase (*theosebēs*) and its relative, *theisebeia* (1 Tim. 2:10), refer to general religious piety. The man who had been healed of his blindness told the Pharisees that Jesus was a prophet. The Pharisees challenged him by saying that they knew that Moses was sent from God but did not know where Jesus had come from. The man replied that everyone knew that if a person is a *theosebēs* (one who has true piety toward God) and does God's will, God hears him. Since God heard Jesus, and healed the man of blindness, Jesus obviously was a *theosebēs* (a truly pious man); and a truly pious man is from God. Thus, the Pharisees were put to silence by a lowly, presumably unschooled man newly healed from blindness. Indeed, he used their own brand of logic to confound them. God truly uses "the foolish things of the world to confound the wise" (1 Cor. 1:27).

NASB: if anyone is God-fearing
NIV: He listens to the godly man
NKJV, RSV: but if anyone is a worshiper of God
LB: those who worship him

151
and **wrapped him in swaddling clothes** (Luke 2:7)
GREEK: *kai esparganōsen auton*

This clause appears only in Luke 2:7, although the verb appears in v. 12 in participial form. The clause is introduced by the conjunction *kai* ("and") followed by the verb *esparganōsen* (in the aorist indicative), followed by the direct object, the masculine pronoun *auton* ("him"). In the Near East, starting from ancient times, it was customary to wrap and restrain infants. Newborns were generally washed immediately after birth, rubbed with salt, and wrapped fairly tightly in pieces of cloth (see Job 38:8-9; Ezek 16:4). As far as is known, swaddling consisted of placing the newborn on a piece of cloth, which was then folded around the body and bound with strips of cloth to make a sort of bundle. The single word *esparganōsen* literally means "to wrap up in infant clothes." The verb appears in the Septuagint (Greek Old Testament) in Job 38:9 and Ezek. 16:4 for the Hebrew *ḥātūllāh* and its root *ḥātal* ("to wrap" or "entwine"). Another derivative of *ḥātal* (translated "bandage") occurs in Ezek. 30:21 and has been found in Ugaritic.

The diapering and dressing of newborns has, of course, been virtually universal in all times, but there is little consistency among the translations of *esparganōsen*. Neither the Latin Vulgate nor the Gothic tried to translate, but simply paraphrased. The words "swaddle" and "to swaddle" are purely English and appear as early as 1200. Wycliffe (1380), however, rendered "a yunge child wrappid in clothis"—close to the Vulgate's *et panniseum involvit*. But Tyndale (1534) translated "the chylde swadled," the same basic phrase used in several contemporary English versions of the Job and Ezekiel passages. Coverdale (1539) altered the reading to "the chylde wrapped in swadling clothes," but the Geneva Version of 1557 returned to the verbal "swaddle."

An interesting aside is recorded in the Journal of Charles Wesley for 1747, in which he mentions that the early Methodists sometimes were called "swaddlers" by their detractors.

NASB: wrapped Him in cloths
NIV: wrapped him in cloths
NKJV: wrapped Him in swaddling cloths
RSV: wrapped him in swaddling clothes
LB: wrapped him in a blanket (note: Lit., "swaddling clothes")

Y

152
Ye shall not surely die (Gen. 3:4)
HEBREW: *lōʾ-môt tᵉmūtûn*

This very important phrase occurs only in Gen. 3:4, in the dialogue between Eve and the serpent. The temptation began with the serpent's questioning God's command to Adam. The poetic structure is as follows:

> And he said unto the woman,
> Yea, hath God said,
> Ye shall not eat
> Of any tree of the garden?

Eve replied that they could eat of all the fruit trees but not of the tree in the midst of the garden (the tree of the knowledge of good and evil). The serpent answered in a two-line poetic stanza:

> And the Serpent said unto the woman,
> Ye shall not surely die.

The literary form of this reply is rather rare, as it consists of the negative particle *lōʾ* attached to but one verb, in the base stem, futuritive form. The purpose of this construction is to express strong contrast, or antithesis, to another verb. Usually the negative particle comes between the two verbal elements, as in Jer. 13:12, "Do we not certainly know" (*hayādoʿa lōʾ nēdaʿ*) and Jer. 30:11, "[I] will not leave thee altogether unpunished" (*wᵉnaqqēh lōʾ ʾănaqqekkā*). A more literal translation would therefore be: "You shall by no certainty die," or even stronger, "You shall by no means die." It is therefore the certainty of death, rather than the fact of death, that the serpent questions. The continual human longing has since been to somehow beat the laws of existence, the very creation ordinance, rather than obey the commands of God.

NASB: You surely shall not die!
NIV, NKJV: You will not surely die

RSV: You will not die
LB: That's a lie! ... You'll not die!

U. Cassuto, *A Commentary on Genesis*, pt. 1 (Jerusalem: Hebrew U. Press, 1961), p. 145.

153
ye that fear God (Acts 13:16)
  GREEK: *hoi phoboumenoi ton theon*

This phrase distinguishes a group of people from the preceding "Men of Israel." It consists of the definite article (vocative), the participle, and the direct object (*theon*) of the participle preceded by its definite article. The phrase also appears in Acts 10:2, 22, cf. 35; 13:26. God-fearers were a class of proselytes distinct from full proselytes—Gentiles who were related to the synagogue but who had not fully become Jews. There is evidence that even official recognition of Judaism was widespread—including the persistent story that many Hellenistic Gentile rulers supported the translation of the Septuagint (Greek Old Testament).

The god-fearer Cornelius (Acts 10:2, 22) was not circumcised, for Peter explains that although it was unlawful for a Jew to associate with a foreigner (Gentile) or even visit him, God had commanded him to come to Cornelius and his household (Acts 10:28). When Peter returned to Jerusalem, news of his activities preceded him and those of the circumcision party (legalistic Jewish Christians) opposed him for visiting and eating with uncircumcised men such as Cornelius and his relatives (Acts 11:3).

Such partial converts were also called *sebomenoi ton theon* ("worshipers of God"; q.v.). Hence, "fear" meant not so much dread of God the judge as showing Him proper reverence and obedience as Lord (see Ps. 15:4; Mal. 3:16). Our phrase therefore means "those who reverence God," or, in its fuller connotation, "those who worship God."

NASB, NKJV: you who fear God
NIV: you Gentiles who worship God
RSV: you that fear God
LB: all others ... who reverence God

Scripture Index

(Numbers in the right-hand column refer to numbered *articles*, not pages)

Genesis		8:21	37, 122	28:22	63
1–2	36	9	15	29:17	93
1:1	50, 59, 65	9:6	65	32:28	18
1:2	50	9:13	15	32:30	39
1:5	17	9:25	72	34:31	103
1:20	43	10:1	127	35:11	20
1:21	65	10:10	77	36:1	127
1:26	50, 65	11:2	77	36:9	127
1:26-27	66	11:4	88	37:2	127
1:27	65	11:10	127	37:34	106
1:28	75	11:27	127	38:7	37
2:7	83	11:28	137	38:8	62
2:8	48	11:31	137	38:14-15	103
2:10	48	12:1	50	39:7	82
2:17	63, 133	12:2	88	40:17	109
2:19	17	12:3	64	42:5	18
3	48	12:7	110	43:3	63
3:1	65	13:10	48	49:8-9	136
3:3	133	13:14	82	50:26	4
3:5	133	14:1	77		
3:15	69	14:9	77	**Exodus**	
3:20	17	14:18-20	96, 109	1:28	15
3:21	19	17:8	50	2:3	4
3:22,	132, 133	18	35	3:2	3
3:23-24	48	18:10	63	4:11	115
3:24	132	18:18	63	4:12	115
4–6	110	19	35	4:15	115
4:1	37, 39, 56, 75, 84	19:5	75	4:22	44
4:16	48	19:8	75	6:3	37, 39, 56
5:1	127	19:14	87	6:3-8	84
5:6	116	19:26	22	6:4	56
5:29	17	22:11	3	7:3	57
6–8	4	22:17	63	8:15	57
6:4	116	23:4	121	9:12	57
6:5	37	24:43	141	9:16-17	57
6:8	37	25:12	127	9:18	57
6:9	127	25:19	127	10:20	57
6:20	83	26:24	112	10:27	57
7:14	83	27:3	15	11:10	57

Subject Index

(All numbers refer to *numbered articles,* not pages)

Selected Bibliography

Aistleitner, Joseph. *Worterbuch der Ugaritischen Sprache*, 4th ed. Berlin: Akademie Verlag, 1974.

Arndt, W. F., and Gingrich, F. W. *A Greek-English Lexicon of the New Testament.* Chicago: University of Chicago Press, 1957.

Barr, James. *The Semantics of Biblical Language.* Oxford: Oxford University Press, 1961.

Barth, J. *Die Nominalbildung in den Semitischen Sprache*, 2d ed. Leipzig, 1894. Reprint. Wiesbaden: O. Harrassowitz, 1961.

Bauer, H., and Leander, P. *Historische Grammatik in den Semitischen Sprachen*, 2d ed. Halle: Universiteit Verlag, 1922.

Bergstrasser, B. *Hebraische Grammatik.* Vols. 1-2. Leipzig, 1918. Reprint. Hildesheim: G. Olms, 1962.

Black, Matthew. *An Aramaic Approach to the Gospels and Acts.* Oxford: Clarendon Press, 1946.

Botterweck, G. J., and Ringgren, Helmer. *Theological Dictionary of the Old Testament.* Grand Rapids: Eerdmans, 1974.

Broekelmann, C. *Grundriss der Vergleichenden Grammatik der Semitischen Sprachen.* Vols. 1-2. Berlin, 1908, 1913. Reprint. Hildesheim: G. Olms, 1959.

Brown, Francis; Driver, S. R.; and Briggs, Charles A. *A Hebrew and English Lexicon of the Old Testament.* Oxford: Oxford University Press, 1907.

Burton, E. De Witt. *Syntax of the Moods and Tenses in New Testament Greek.* Edinburgh: T. & T. Clark, 1898.

Cremer, Herman. *Biblical-Theological Lexicon of New Testament Greek.* New York: Charles Scribner's Sons, 1895.

Einspahr, Bruce. *Index to Brown, Driver and Briggs Hebrew Lexicon.* Chicago: Moody Press, 1976.

Gesenius, F. H. W. *Hebrew Grammar*, 2d ed. Edited by E. Kautzsch and A. E. Cowley. Oxford: Clarendon Press, 1910.

Girdlestone, R. B. *Synonyms of the Old Testament*, 2d ed. London, 1897. Reprint. Grand Rapids: Eerdmans, 1960.

Han, Nathan E. *A Parsing Guide to the Greek New Testament.* Scottdale, Pa: Herald Press, 1971.

Harris, R. Laird; Archer, Gleason L., Jr.; and Waltke, Bruce K. *Theological Wordbook of the Old Testament.* 2 vols. Chicago: Moody Press, 1980.

Koehler, L., and Baumgartner, W. *Lexicon in Veteris Testamenti Libros*, 2d ed., German-English. Leiden: E.J. Brill, 1958. 3d ed. in progress.

Samuel, Lee, ed. *Biblia Sacra Polyglotta*, 2 vols. London: Bagster, 1831.

Lisowsky, Gerhard. *Konkordanz zum Hebraischen Alten Testament.* 2d ed., *Wurtembergische Bibelanstalt.* Stuttgart: Privileg, 1958. Available through the United Bible Societies.

Mandelkern, Solomon. *Concordance on the Bible (Hebrew).* 2 vols. Leipzig, 1896. Numerous reprints. New York: Shulzinger Bros., 1961.

Moulton, J. H.; Howard, W. F.; and Turner, N. *A Grammar of New Testament Greek.* 3 vols. Edinburgh: T. & T. Clark, 1906-1963.

Moulton, J., and Milligan, G. *The Vocabulary of the Greek Testament.* Grand Rapids: Eerdmans, 1950.

Pettinato, G. *The Archives of Ebla.* New York: Doubleday, 1981.

Rienecker, Fritz. *Sprachlicher Schlussel zum Griechischen Neuen Testament.* Giessen-Basel, 1956.

Robertson, A. T. *A Grammar of the Greek New Testament in the Light of Historical Research.* Nashville: Broadman, 1934.

Schleusner, J. F. *Novus Thesaurus Philologico-Criticus sive Lexicon in LXX Veteris Testamenti.* 3 vols. Glasgow: Read & Son, 1822.

Tenney, Merrill C., ed. *The New Pictorial Encyclopedia of the Bible.* Grand Rapids: Zondervan, 1975.

Turner, Nigel. *Christian Words.* Nashville: Nelson, 1982.

_____. *Grammatical Insights into the New Testament.* Edinburgh: T. & T. Clark, 1966.

Unger, Merrill F., and White, William, Jr., eds. *Nelson's Expository Dictionary of the Old Testament.* Nashville: Nelson, 1980.

Ximenes, Francisco. *Biblia Polyglotta.* 6 vols. Complutum, Spain: Industria Arnaldi Guillelmi de Brocario, in Academica Complutensi, 1514-17.